Critical acclaim for the first edition of *The Tallest Tower*

"An interesting story interestingly told, and as such it is welcome . . . offers a particularly clear description of Eiffel's engineering principles, skillfully woven into the narrative." — *The New York Times*

"Fascinating and highly instructive . . . a book not to miss." —Janet Flanner, Paris correspondent, *The New Yorker*

"A comprehensive account of the man who designed and built [the tower], the period out of which it came and the significance it has assumed in art, engineering and architecture. The book is written with wit and charm." — *Los Angeles Times*

"This volume is a delightful illustrated social history of the tower . . . telling the full story of the structure, so intricately twined with contemporary history." — *Scientific American*

"Mr. Harriss has told the tower's story with conscientious zest, packing his account with anecdotes and historic details." — *The Christian Science Monitor*

"Certainly the best biography of a building and the cultural climate which spawned it we've read in a very long time." — *Kirkus Reviews*

"Harriss succeeds admirably . . . This is a well-organized, exceptionally readable book; entertaining, informative, and highly recommended." — *Library Journal*

"Marvelously evocative portrait of Gustave Eiffel and the technological daring, engineering know-how, and romantic vision which have made his tower a landmark." —American Library Association *Booklist*

"Pleasant, thorough book . . . the Eiffel Tower emerges as a vibrant flagstaff to freedom, a scientific testing ground, a gigantic frivolity and a surprising aesthetic triumph." — *Publishers Weekly*

The Tallest Tower

An early promotional illustration of the Eiffel Tower before its construction.
(Collection Tour Eiffel)

The Tallest Tower

New Edition, Revised and Updated

Joseph Harriss

Unlimited Publishing
Bloomington, Indiana

To the memory of my father, an engineer.

Contents

The Tallest Tower

Prologue

ONE EVENING I took a random stroll on the Champ de Mars, not far from my home in Paris. After walking for a while, I found myself beneath the Eiffel Tower and glanced up. Above me the colossal, intricate, overarching tracery of crisscrossing girders soared more majestically than the columns of any gothic cathedral. Although I had looked at the tower countless times during my years as a Paris-based journalist, this time I *saw* it. I was held, fascinated—awe-struck is not too strong a word. I decided to find out more about this odd, captivating structure. I learned that the tower was not merely a fairground gimmick, but the all-but-inevitable outgrowth of an era, in some ways the epitome of an age.

In France, that age coincided with the country's third, precarious attempt at democracy in the space of less than a century, after its long history of monarchy and empire. The Third Republic was conceived in the confused aftermath of France's humiliating defeat by the Prussians in 1870. The era ended 69 years and 107 French governments later, in the debacle of France's abject capitulation to Nazi Germany in 1940. Between those worst of times, however, many French citizens lived in what may have been one of the best of times.

The Belle Epoque, like the Renaissance and other neat labels bestowed by historians, was not a pat, monolithic era. It was a tumultuous time of tension and contradiction, change and anticipation—and, yes, even terrorism—much like our own. But it does appear that there was a period toward the end of the 19th century when new prosperity and old values fused briefly to produce an era in many ways happier, or at least less riddled with doubt and anxiety, than any we have known since.

This was the age that, with a remarkable sense of itself, created the Eiffel Tower. A synthesis of technology and mood, this bizarre construction was a compendium of engineering methods and materials developed during the first century of the Industrial Revolution. It was also, it seems to me, the most expressive statement of how one part of the human race felt about itself at a pivotal point in its history.

A Fair for France

THE FRENCH WERE not alone in enjoying the momentary state of grace known as the Belle Epoque. Most of northwestern Europe and the northeastern United States experienced it in recognizably similar form—the Gay Nineties. But if France's euphoria in the last years of the 19th century appears heightened, the impression is perhaps due to a backdrop of travail. For the Franco-Prussian War, in which the Imperial Army of Napoleon III was smashed in a matter of weeks, was not merely a military defeat.

The war led to the loss of France's large eastern provinces of Alsace and Lorraine, with a population of nearly a million and a half, economically vital mines and industries, and the great city of Strasbourg. Moreover, the settlement that President Adolphe Thiers made with the Germans in February 1871 involved an enormous and debilitating indemnity of five billion francs, or about one billion dollars. It also stipulated that German troops would occupy the country's eastern region until the sum had been paid.[1]

Parisians in particular had borne much of the brunt of the war, undergoing a five-month siege during which they were reduced to eating cats, rats, and the animals in their zoos. No sooner had peace been concluded than the revolt of the Paris Commune broke out on March 18. A political insurrection in the image of those that had shaken Paris sporadically for a century, the Commune revolt was sparked when President Thiers suspended payment to national guardsmen—the only income of many families because of severe unemployment at the time—and ended a moratorium on rents and bills.

Moreover, Parisians felt increasingly isolated and misunderstood when the National Assembly moved to Versailles to escape the seething resentment in the capital. The national guardsmen of

Montmartre and Belleville, on the north side of Paris, refused to yield their weapons, including over 200 cannons, when ordered to disarm. They proclaimed the independent, self-governing Commune of Paris, and for two months the city was ravaged by fire and divided by barricades as 30,000 Communards held out against 130,000 government troops. When Marshal MacMahon's army finally quelled the revolt after bloody street fighting, nearly 20,000 Parisians had died at the hands of their compatriots. Entire areas of the city lay in ruin.

As the stunned city began to put itself back together, it first had to overcome its own divisive tendencies. Of the National Assembly elected in 1871, nearly 400 of its 650 members were monarchists dedicated to ending the country's democratic form of government as soon as they could decide who would be king. Unable to choose among the Comte de Chambord, the Comte de Paris and a possible Bonaparte, however, the Assembly reluctantly gave birth to the Third Republic.

France's third stab at democracy since the revolution of 1789 came about not due to any real consensus that it was the best form of government, but only because, as President Thiers said later, "It divided us least."[2] Inevitably, a period of political confusion began—there would be 12 governments over the next eight years alone—but the Republic survived. Ironically, the nation's most conservative elements, the peasantry and the haute bourgeoisie, would preserve it against the right-wing monarchists.

France went to work on its problems. First of all it paid off the indemnity much more rapidly than anyone had foreseen, thanks to the enthusiastic response of French investors to the government's bond issues. By July 1871, France had paid Germany enough for German troops to be evacuated from five of 21 occupied eastern departments. The remaining soldiers left in September 1873, a year ahead of schedule; by 1875 France had already balanced its budget.

It began healing its self-inflicted wounds as well. In 1879 the government felt secure enough to make "The Marseillaise" the national anthem, and to move the Chamber of Deputies and the Senate back to Paris from Versailles. It granted a full amnesty in 1880 to the thousands of Communard prisoners or exiles.

As the economy gained momentum, the standard of living improved rapidly. National income nearly doubled in the four decades following 1870; industrial production tripled and foreign trade increased 75 percent. To the chagrin of German geologists who in 1871 had laid out the boundaries of Lorraine in such a way as to annex all known iron deposits, France discovered it had the largest iron vein in Europe on its side of the border, reserves estimated at almost one-fifth of the world's total supply. During the 1880s, France gradually conquered a colonial empire in Indochina and North and Central Africa that was to become second only to Great Britain's in terms of population and size. The colonies would also be an enormous new market for French investment and industrial output.

Altogether, it was an amazing comeback. With democracy firmly established and the nation once again a prosperous world power, the government began looking forward to commemorating the centennial of the French Revolution. As early as 1878, several cabinet ministers were gestating the idea of a purely national industrial fair to be held in 1889.[3]

In truth, the government was worried about celebrating the anniversary too ostentatiously. France was already considered with suspicion by the rest of monarchical Europe as a regicidal upstart, a hotbed of bloody republicanism. It would be best, some timorous officials argued, to mark the centennial *en famille*, and not disturb neighboring crowned heads with an international celebration of revolution. Besides, they feared that invitations to exhibit at a world's fair held to commemorate 1789 might be met with contemptuous rebuffs from the monarchies.

Prime Minister Jules Ferry, an outspoken, energetic believer in democracy who as minister of education had made free secular schooling compulsory, and as prime minister had been one of the chief promoters of France's colonial expansion, thought otherwise. He favored a world's fair as a vehicle for demonstrating France's newly recovered place in the sun, touting her industrial might, commercial success and engineering savvy.

He ultimately prevailed, and on November 8, 1884, President Jules Grévy signed a brief decree ordering that "A Universal

Exposition of the Products of Industry shall be opened in Paris May 5, 1889, and closed October 31 following." Neither Grévy nor even the audacious Ferry could foresee that this would be the biggest, most varied, and most spectacularly successful world's fair ever held until that time.

THE INDUSTRIAL FAIR was an invention of the 19th century, and therefore an especially apt form for the centennial of 1789. Paris and London had used such fairs throughout the century as showcases for their progress as they vied for first place in Europe. Occasionally the rivalry sharpened to reflect a state of heightened tension, as at France's fair in 1798, sponsored by the Directory while Bonaparte's armies battled the British. "The participant who can show that his products and trade have dealt the worst blow to English industry will receive a gold medal," the government promised.[4]

In general, however, the competition was more gentlemanly. This was in keeping with the cosmopolitan spirit of Europe's fairs dating back to the important ones of France's Champagne region in the 12th century, which brought together the best products from around the world: Flemish and English fabrics, German linens, Russian furs, spices from the Orient. The two annual fairs at Troyes, 100 miles east of Paris, assumed such importance that "troy weights" of pounds and ounces became a standard international measure.

The first nation to enter the industrial era was also the first to hold an industrial world's fair, when Britain's Prince Albert invited all "civilized" nations to an exhibition that opened in London's Hyde Park on May 1, 1851. Over 13,000 participants responded, nearly half of them non-British. The fair's main attraction was Joseph Paxton's colossal Crystal Palace. An airy bubble of glass with iron ribs, the Palace had nearly 1 million square feet of floor space and was the largest enclosure yet constructed, prefiguring the innovative use of iron later in the century.[5] The fair was seen by over 6 million visitors and set a standard for international exhibitions that followed.[6]

France took up the gauntlet and inaugurated a series of world's fairs at roughly eleven-year intervals beginning in 1855 and reaching its climax in 1900. Although London never again mounted an exhibition to match the Crystal Palace, Paris progressed from one success to another. Its first *Palais de l'Industrie*, or Machinery Hall, a cathedral of commerce with a glass and iron central nave twice as wide as that of the Crystal Palace, gave notice in 1855 of things to come. An attendance record of 15 million was set at the Paris fair of 1867. This rose to 16 million in 1878, and shot to over 32 million in 1889, as Victorian enthusiasm for the era's wondrous new machines grew apace.

The organizers of the Paris Exposition of 1889 soft-pedaled its role as the centennial celebration of the French Revolution out of consideration for aristocratic sensibilities both at home and abroad. (In France itself, the Republic was still contemptuously called *la gueuse*, the slut, by monarchists; titled folk defiantly shuttered their windows every July 14 to block the vulgar noise of Bastille Day festivities.)

Sensitive political implications were de-emphasized in the prospectus prepared in March 1885 by the government study committee. "The Exposition of 1889," it stated with all due political correctness, "will have the character of a centennial exhibit, summing up what freedom of work has produced in terms of progress during the past hundred years. The year 1789 was a historic date in economics as well as politics, and it is to examine the world's economic situation that all nations are invited."[7]

All nations were not entirely convinced that the basic significance of France's centennial was economic. Several monarchies, including Austria-Hungary, Belgium, Britain and Holland refused official participation in the fair. Private interests eventually organized their exhibits. Germany, reflecting the continuing tension with a France dedicated to regaining Alsace and Lorraine, remained pointedly aloof.

With governmental instability hampering plans for the fair—Ferry's replacement as prime minister, Henri Brisson, lasted only nine months—the project did not really begin taking shape until the spring of 1886, only three years before the official opening date. A second wind was provided in part by the new minister of commerce and industry, Edouard Lockroy, one of the more original cabinet members to serve the Third Republic.

A graduate of the Beaux-Arts school of art, author of several comedies and operettas, sometime journalist, Lockroy was a *littérateur* who moved in the same circles as Victor Hugo and was known for his biting wit. The fair caught his fancy, and he pushed through its budget of $8.6 million to be provided by the government, the City of Paris, and a private company founded to underwrite the project. It was also Lockroy who, casting about for an appropriate, Babel-like symbol for the fair, took up and promoted the idea of a thousand-foot tower.

The notion was not particularly new. In fact, it was in the air on both sides of the Atlantic as the nations that had been the first to realize the early potential of the Industrial Revolution looked for ways to dramatize their new prowess and prosperity. It was as if they were obeying a compulsion constant throughout history to thrust mighty structures toward the sky in moments of special pride: in legend the Tower of Babel, in reality the Great Pyramid of Cheops and the medieval cathedrals.

The difference in the 19th century was that whereas the pretext, at least, for such previous exercises nearly always had been religious, the new secular faith in material progress justified an engineering feat for its own sake. Actually, 1889 marked the centenary of what a British historian, E. J. Hobsbawm, has called the Dual Revolution that transformed Europe: the French Revolution, which provided the seminal political and social ideology for the Western world, and the Industrial Revolution, which seemingly furnished the means to attain liberty, equality, and fraternity.

Confidence in progress and human perfectibility then was a peak that from our disabused, postindustrial perspective appears touchingly naïve. As Georges Berger, the ebullient general manager of the Exposition of 1889, expressed its grand goal:

> We will show our sons what their fathers have accomplished in the space of a century through progress in knowledge, love of work and respect for liberty. We will give them a view from the

summit of the steep slope that has been climbed since the dark ages. And if one day they should again descend to some valley of error and misery, they will remember what we did and they will remind their children of it, and future generations will thereby be more determined than ever to climb still higher than we have. For the law of progress is immortal, just as progress itself is infinite.[8]

As early as March 1833, the great British railroad engineer Richard Trevithick had proposed a thousand-foot tower for London to commemorate passage of Britain's First Reform Act, which had created a more equitable distribution of seats in Parliament and added half-a-million voters to the lists. The structure was to have been of cast iron, 100 feet in diameter at the base and 10 feet across at the top, surmounted by a colossal statue. Trevithick died in April of that year, however, and his idea was not acted upon by King William IV.

The idea continued to fascinate engineers. In 1874, two Americans, Clarke and Reeves, drew up plans for a thousand-foot iron tower for the Philadelphia Centennial Exposition of 1876. The cylinder was to be only 30 feet in diameter, braced by cables attached to a circular masonry base. The exposition's organizers rejected what must have resembled a glorified factory chimney.

The most ambitious tower actually to be erected before 1889 was the Washington Monument. But this 555-foot, all-masonry obelisk completed in 1884 was far smaller than the thousand-foot tower that had become a virtual obsession of 19th-century engineers.

Therefore when Edouard Lockroy considered how to give the Paris Exposition of 1889 special *éclat*, a thousand-foot tower was the obvious choice. In the notice published in the government's *Journal Officiel* of May 2, 1886, French architects and engineers bidding to construct the fair's semi-permanent buildings and other attractions were invited to "study the possibility of erecting on the Champ de Mars an iron tower with a base 125 meters square and 300 meters tall. If they consider it desirable they may present a different plan without such a tower." It was no coincidence that 300 meters, or 986 feet, was the nearest round metric equivalent to a thousand feet. And despite the admissibility of designs omitting a tower, it was clear that Lockroy wanted one.

With time running short, contestants had only 16 days in which to draw up their initial blueprints. Over 100 projects came in by the May 18 deadline. The projects were shown to the public for three days and considered by Lockroy's Exposition committee for five days before winners of the 12 prizes, ranging from the equivalent of $800 to $200, were announced.

Working hastily, the committee rejected out of hand dozens of perfervidly inventive projects. One designer proposed a tower in the form of a gigantic garden sprinkler which could be used, he claimed, to water Paris in case of drought. Another envisioned an immense guillotine to symbolize the Revolution. One apparently valid idea was a tower bestriding the Seine at the Iéna Bridge, linking the Champ de Mars and the Trocadéro gardens. This plan was finally disqualified because of the danger of laying foundations for a tower of several thousand tons directly on the riverbed. Besides, official criteria required that the tower be on the Champ de Mars itself.

Another intriguing proposal described a thousand-foot tower with a powerful electric light at its summit. A system of parabolic mirrors would reflect light so efficiently from the tower at its proposed site on the Esplanade des Invalides to all parts of Paris that even the most remote neighborhoods of the city would receive, as the engineers confidently put it, "eight times as much light as is necessary to read a newspaper." Night, in other words, would be banished from the City of Light. Moreover, the all-granite *Tour Soleil* would be composed of six levels with 15 rooms on each, to be used for "aerotherapy treatments" where the sick would benefit from air as pure as that in the Alps. The tower's hollow center would allow for scientific experiments involving falling objects, and a basement 215 feet deep would house a multistory museum dedicated to electricity. The structure was to be topped off by a 180-foot allegorical statue representing Science.[9]

If Lockroy's committee finally selected Gustave Eiffel's proposal for a tower of iron weighing approximately 7,000 tons and costing the equivalent of $1.6 million, it was partly because of Eiffel's unequaled prestige at 53 years of age as France's master builder in metal, partly because his project was the most practicable in light

Gustave Eiffel in 1889.

of official criteria—but mainly because those criteria apparently were established with Eiffel's design specifically in mind.[10]

His project had in fact been on paper since the latter part of 1884. Prompted by official talk of the Exposition of 1889, Maurice Koechlin, Eiffel's chief of research at Eiffel and Company, in cooperation with another engineer, Emile Nouguier, and the company's architect, Stephan Sauvestre, began initial studies for a tower in June of that year. Koechlin, a Swiss-naturalized Alsatian who had graduated from the prestigious Federal Polytechnic School in Zurich, actually designed the Eiffel Tower.

This fact has occasionally stirred up teapot tempests, mainly in Swiss newspapers, over whether Eiffel stole the idea for the tower from Koechlin. As it happened, Eiffel always gave full credit to Koechlin for the part he played in the initial conception of the tower, and in later life Koechlin never claimed more in the speeches he made on the subject. The project was a company effort: the research bureau turned out several versions of a thousand-foot tower and Eiffel chose the one he considered most likely. He assumed full responsibility for its execution.

Eiffel's project as presented to the Exposition committee. (Photo RMN)

Eiffel's project first became public in December 1884, when it was outlined in a French civil engineering review and in a daily newspaper, *La France*. The following May, Eiffel mentioned the proposal in an address to the French Society of Civil Engineers. Shortly afterward, Eiffel called on Lockroy and presented the tower as a centerpiece for the Exposition of 1889. His success in selling the idea can be seen in the criteria later laid down by Lockroy, who formulated them along the lines of Eiffel's proposal, including a base precisely 125 meters square.

Moreover, while the competition was still going on, Lockroy named a subcommittee on May 12 to study the technical feasibility of Eiffel's iron structure. When the group met on June 12, the fix was in. "The subcommittee rejected several projects as unrealistic," notes the official history of the Exposition of 1889, "several others as insufficiently thorough, and finally decided unanimously that the tower to be erected at the Universal Exposition of 1889 should have a well-defined character and appear as an original masterpiece of the metals industry, and that only the Eiffel Tower seemed to fulfill these requirements." The subcommittee recommended adoption of Eiffel's proposal on condition that further study be given to the particularly complex questions of the tower's elevators and protection from lightning.

Eiffel, an energetic entrepreneur, had stolen a march on the competition by getting to Lockroy first, but he had also presented a compelling case, demolishing in the process the notion that a thousand-foot tower could be built of masonry. A stone tower of such height, he argued, would present special problems concerning settling of its foundations, cohesion of mortar under unprecedented pressures, and the construction time required if traditional methods were used. Building in stone had reached the limit of its technology: "Antiquity, the Middle Ages and the Renaissance have pushed the use of stone to the extreme," he reasoned, "and it hardly appears possible to go further than our predecessors have with the same materials, especially since masonry construction techniques have not progressed notably for some time."[11]

He pointed out that the world's tallest stone structure, the Washington Monument, was only 555 feet tall, and the age's other monuments, particularly Europe's soaring cathedral spires, were still smaller: Cologne Cathedral, for instance, reached only 512 feet, Rouen was 492 feet, and Chartres 370 feet. Saint Paul's dome in London rose 361 feet, and the dome of Washington's Capitol was 305 feet high. Clearly, new ambitions called for new materials and techniques.

That meant cast iron, wrought iron or steel, the metals that had revolutionized 19th century construction techniques, enabling engineers to meet the urgent demands of the railroads for hundreds of bridges, train sheds, and other infrastructure. Cast iron, brittle and lacking tensile strength, was suitable only in the same compressive role as stone, for columns and arches. Steel, on the other hand, was lighter and more flexible, perhaps too much so for the tower Eiffel had in mind; he feared that steel's greater elasticity would produce an intolerable amount of sway in high winds. Steel also was considerably more costly, since it was just then coming into mass production.[12]

Thus his project was a wrought-iron structure that would combine strength with rigidity and still be relatively light. Moreover, Eiffel held out the possibility of dismantling his iron tower if the City of Paris so desired at a later date, an option administrators would not have with a masonry structure.

Eiffel's authoritative arguments were buttressed by his long experience in iron construction. He had been building railway bridges and a host of other metal structures in France and around the world for 30 years. He now claimed to have devised a system of lattice-trussed piers with incurving edges that theoretically made it possible to construct towers of virtually any height. The Exposition committee was willing to gamble that he was right.

"Useless and Monstrous"

On January 8, 1887, seven months after the Exposition subcommittee voted in favor of Eiffel's bid, Edouard Lockroy and the City of Paris signed a contract with Eiffel. The engineer agreed to construct a thousand-foot tower corresponding to his proposal in time for the opening of the Exposition of 1889. He was to receive a subsidy of the equivalent of $300,000 at the time in three installments, the last due on the date of completion. He was also given a franchise to operate the tower and to open restaurants, cafes and other attractions on it during the fair and for the following 20 years, after which full ownership would return to the City of Paris.[1]

To anyone but the supremely confident Eiffel, the undertaking would have appeared foolhardy, questions of the basic wisdom of creating such an eccentric structure aside. For one thing, the committee had procrastinated to the point where a scant two years remained in which to construct the tallest tower ever conceived. No guiding precedent existed. The Washington Monument had taken no less than 36 years from cornerstone to capstone, including time lost due to financial and technical problems. And the subsidy granted by the French government covered less than one-fifth of the tower's projected cost. Eiffel was to provide the remainder, the equivalent of $1.3 million, with the possibility of recovering his investment if the tower turned out a financial success.

But there was no question now of turning back. France had announced to the world the most complete, the most dazzling world's fair ever held. Its symbol and centerpiece had to be the thousand-foot tower that seemed the inevitable technical apotheosis of the century.

For three more weeks, the Exposition committee indulged its proclivity for dither while it considered where, exactly, the tower should stand. Members wondered whether the initial choice of location at the end of the Champ de Mars near the Seine might not spoil the area's proportions. Perhaps the tower would be set off to advantage by being placed atop Mont Valérien, a few miles to the west, rather than a low point near the river. Or perhaps, they fretted, such a distinctive monument installed permanently in the area would intrude on subsequent fairs with different architecture and layout.

Financial considerations finally dictated that the tower be close enough to the fairgrounds that both the fair and the tower would benefit from their combined appeal to the public. Also, on the Champ de Mars the tower's gigantic arches would have the additional role of monumental entrance to the fair—saving the government the cost of constructing one. As the French say, there are no small savings.

The final decision made, workers began digging the tower's foundations on January 26, 1887. There was never any doubt in Eiffel's mind that he was engaged in a historic enterprise. It was his intention, he said, "to raise to the glory of modern science, and to the greater honor of French industry, an arch of triumph as striking as those that preceding generations had raised to conquerors."[2]

The tower's immediate symbolic importance for France and, in particular, for the Exposition of 1889, was spelled out by Alfred Picard, official historian of the fair: "This colossal work was to constitute a brilliant manifestation of the industrial strength of our country, attest to the immense progress realized in the art of metal structures, celebrate the unprecedented progress of civil engineering during the course of this century, attract multitudes of visitors, and contribute largely to the success of the great peaceful commemoration of the centenary of 1789." Eventually, and not altogether incidentally, the tower was also to make a great deal of money.

But before that, even before its construction had got well under way, the tower was to make a number of people angry. *Le tout*

Paris had been talking for months of Eiffel's project, mostly with the boulevardier's amused skepticism. When the first cubic yards of earth began to leave the Champ de Mars, however, it became clear that the mad thing would actually be attempted.

The technical feasibility of a thousand-foot tower necessarily escaped most Parisians' judgment, but its potential effect on the city's skyline did not. Self-appointed tastemakers in this nation that prided itself on being beauty's most devoted acolyte rose up in rage.

Forty-seven of the most righteously indignant penned a letter of protest in early February to Charles Adolphe Alphand, the minister of public works, the government cabinet member ultimately responsible for the Exposition. Redolent of its time and place (and all too typical, some may be tempted to think, of French preening), the *protestation des artistes* is worth savoring in full:

> Writers, painters, sculptors, architects, passionate lovers of the heretofore intact beauty of Paris, we come to protest with all our might, with all our indignation, in the name of betrayed French taste, in the name of threatened French art and history, against the erection in the heart of our capital of the useless and monstrous Eiffel Tower, which the public has scornfully and rightly dubbed the Tower of Babel.
>
> Without being blind chauvinists, we have the right to proclaim publicly that Paris is without rival in the world. Along its streets and wide boulevards, beside its admirable riverbanks, amid its magnificent promenades, stand the most noble monuments to which human genius has ever given birth. The soul of France, the creator of masterpieces, shines among this august proliferation of stone. Italy, Germany, Flanders, so rightly proud of their artistic heritage, possess nothing comparable to ours, and Paris attracts curiosity and admiration from all corners of the universe. Are we to let all that be profaned? Is the City of Paris to associate itself any longer with the baroque, mercantile imaginings of a builder of machines, and thus dishonor and disfigure itself irreparably? For the Eiffel Tower, which even commercial America would not have, is without a doubt the dishonor of Paris. Everyone feels it, everyone says it, everyone is profoundly saddened by it, and we are only a weak echo of public opinion so legitimately alarmed. When

foreigners visit our Exposition they will cry out in astonishment, "Is it this horror that the French have created to give us an idea of their vaunted taste?" They will be right to mock us, for the Paris of sublime gothic, the Paris of Jean Goujon, of Germain Pilon, of Puget, of Rude, of Barye, etc., will have become the Paris of Monsieur Eiffel.

For that matter, all one must do to understand our case is to imagine for a moment a dizzily ridiculous tower dominating Paris like a black and gigantic factory chimney, crushing beneath its barbarous mass Notre Dame, the Sainte Chapelle, the Tour Saint Jacques, the Louvre, the dome of the Invalides, the Arch of Triumph, all our humiliated monuments, all our raped architecture disappearing in this stupefying dream. And for the next 20 years we will see cast over the entire city, still trembling with the genius of so many centuries, cast like a spot of ink, the odious shadow of the odious column of bolted metal.

It is up to you who so love Paris, who have so beautified it, who have so often protected it against administrative devastation and the vandalism of industry, to defend it once again. We entrust to you the task of pleading the cause of Paris, knowing that you will bring to it all the energy, all the eloquence that the love of the beautiful, the great, the proper inspire in an artist such as yourself. And if our cry of alarm is not heard, if our argument is not listened to, if Paris stubbornly goes ahead with an idea that dishonors Paris, we will at least, you and we, have expressed an honorable protest.[3]

The letter was signed by Ernest Meissonier, the painter, Charles Gounod, composer of the opera *Faust*, Charles Garnier, architect of the Paris Opéra, Adolphe William Bouguereau, a leading painter of the pompous "academic" school, such writers as Alexandre Dumas *fils*, François Coppée, Leconte de Lisle, Sully Prudhomme and Guy de Maupassant, and three dozen lesser lights. Their outrage, though perhaps expressing a laudable concern for protecting the aesthetic environment, was unfortunately typical of the snobbish attitude still prevalent today toward anything that dares be as sheerly *obvious* as the Eiffel Tower.

The writers, especially, continued to heap scorn upon it, unaware that it would eventually become a semi-sacred object of contemplation for a later generation of writers and philosophers.

Maupassant in particular professed boundless contempt for the structure. The possibly apocryphal story is still told in Paris that he frequently lunched at the restaurant on the tower's second platform, because that was the only place in the city where he could be certain not to see it. In his short story, *"La Vie Errante,"* he declares:

> I left Paris and even France because of the Eiffel Tower. Not only is it visible from every point in the city, but it is to be found everywhere, made of every known material, exhibited in every shop window, an unavoidable and tormenting nightmare . . . I wonder what will be thought of our generation if, in some future riot, we do not unbolt this tall, skinny pyramid of iron ladders, this giant and disgraceful skeleton with a base that seems made to support a formidable monument of Cyclops and which aborts into the thin, ridiculous profile of a factory chimney.

He was joined in his dudgeon notably by the morose writer Léon Bloy, who called the tower "a superb hardware shop," and wrote darkly, "I love Paris, the city of intelligence, and I feel Paris threatened by this truly tragic lamppost to which it has given birth, and which will be seen at night from 20 leagues . . . as a distress signal of shipwreck and despair." One can only admire the literary verve and imagery of such vituperation, but despair in this case was in the eye of the beholder, judging by the world's enthusiastic response to the tower for over a century.[4]

As the poet Léon-Paul Fargue, who happened to like the tower, put it later, "when [the tower] came shooting out of the earth, the aesthetes liked it not at all." But this was long before the tower's appeal to the masses led the French National Tourist Office to plead in full-color advertisements, "Do we have to put an Eiffel Tower in every town to get you to appreciate the rest of France?"

Alphand passed the protest on to Lockroy, for whom it was a rare and obviously delightful opportunity to exercise his ironic pen. Ostensibly replying to Alphand but fully expecting his note to get to the Paris newspapers, Lockroy wrote:

Judging by the stately swell of the rhythms, the beauty of the metaphors, the elegance of its delicate and precise style, one can tell without even looking at the signatures that this protest is the result of collaboration of the most famous writers and poets of our time . . . But do not let yourself be impressed by its beautiful form, and note only the facts. The protest is already irrelevant. You will inform the senders that construction of the tower was decided upon a year ago, and that the work site has been open for a month. They could have protested in time: they did not, and "honorable" indignation unfortunately comes a bit late.

I am profoundly sorry about this. Not that I fear for Paris. Notre Dame will remain Notre Dame, and the Arch of Triumph will remain the Arch of Triumph. But I could have saved the only part of this great city which is seriously in danger: that incomparable sandpile called the Champ de Mars, such an inspiration for our poets and so attractive to our landscape painters.

Please express my sorrow to these gentlemen. Above all, do not say that it is unfortunate that the Exposition is being attacked by those who should be defending it; that a protest signed by such illustrious names will echo throughout Europe and may be used as a pretext by some nations not to take part in our celebration; that it is bad to attempt to ridicule a peaceful undertaking that France is so attached to, especially now when she is so unjustly suspected abroad. Such petty considerations concern a cabinet minister, but they are meaningless for rarified minds that are occupied above all with the interests of art and the love of the beautiful.

What I pray you to do is to accept this protest and to keep it. It should be placed in a showcase at the fair. Such beautiful and noble prose cannot but interest the crowds, and perhaps even amaze them.[5]

Lockroy's sarcasm was the perfect parry to the little band of overzealous keepers of the Grail, subjecting them to the one thing they could not stand, public ridicule. They were not heard from again, and several came to be open admirers of the tower.

Before this quintessentially French *affaire* was over, the tower's creator had his say on the subject—an unusual event in an era when engineers were most often considered boors whose aesthetic notions scarcely went beyond the beauty of a neatly placed rivet. In fact, many engineers of the time were simple mechanics of little education, such as James Watt and Thomas Newcomen, whose steam engines were the motive force of the Industrial Revolution. Richard Trevithick had been a carnival strong man and wrestler before trying his hand at locomotives. And Herbert Hoover recalled that in his younger days he had given a nasty shock to an English lady, who shared his table during a trans-Atlantic crossing, by admitting that he was a mining engineer.[6]

Eiffel, however, was a graduate of France's rigorous lycée system, as well as of its proud École Centrale des Arts et Manufactures, one of Europe's first great engineering schools. His sketchbooks filled with pencil drawings indicate an artist's eye and a highly cultivated sensibility. As to the hostile reaction to his tower by part of the artist community, Eiffel viewed the matter with solid Burgundian equanimity and a sure grasp of aesthetics. "I believe that the tower will have its own beauty," he declared in an interview published in the serious daily, *Le Temps.* "The first principle of architectural beauty is that the essential lines of a construction be determined by a perfect appropriateness to its use. What was the main obstacle I had to overcome in designing the tower? Its resistance to wind. And I submit that the curves of its four piers as produced by our calculations, rising from an enormous base and narrowing toward the top, will give a great impression of strength and beauty."

Clearly, the idea that form follows function was not exclusive to the Chicago School of architecture, which was beginning to apply it to the world's first skyscrapers. Interestingly enough in this case, an engineer, not an architect, had articulated the concept. But then Louis Sullivan, the prime mover of modern American architecture and creator of many landmark buildings, himself concluded that the most exciting and original advances of his time in building technique were the work of engineers rather than architects.[7]

"Besides," Eiffel continued, on another tack, "there is an attraction and a charm inherent in the colossal that is not subject to ordinary theories of art. Does anyone pretend that the Pyramids have so forcefully gripped the imagination of men through their artistic value? What are they, after all, but artificial hillocks? And yet what visitor can stand without reaction in their presence? The tower will be the tallest edifice ever raised by man. Will it not therefore be imposing in its own way?"

He concluded on the note that had come to be the leitmotif of the Exposition of 1889, France's emotional need to be taken seriously in the community of nations. "It seems to me that the Eiffel Tower is worthy of being treated with respect, if only because it will show that we are not simply a frivolous people, but also the country of engineers and builders who are called upon all over the world to construct bridges, viaducts, train stations and the great monuments of modern industry."[8]

France had come a long way since its humiliation of 1870, and it intended to prove that to a skeptical world—and coincidentally to itself—with the 1889 world's fair and a tower so tall that other nations had only dreamed of building it. The country was riding the crest of the first wave of industrialism. In a broader sense, the iron tower that was to symbolize France's soaring pride of accomplishment would also signal that a new era, full of incalculable portent, had begun.

Glorious Times for Engineers

THE INDUSTRIAL AGE, which Gustave Eiffel exemplified in his career and celebrated with his tower, was just 50 years old when he was born. Such a statement admittedly is possible only through a willing suspension of disbelief in the distinctness of historical eras.

In this case, historians seem to agree that the Industrial Revolution "occurred" in Great Britain in the 1780s. While there had been in history previous periods of great creativity and relative prosperity, it was during that decade that, thanks to radically new developments in work organization and power production, Britain "took off" into the continuous, self-sustained growth that characterizes an industrial economy.

Other European nations and the United States, informed by the liberating rationalist thought of the 18th-century Enlightenment and poised economically on the verge of takeoff, soon followed. By the 1820s sociologists in Britain and France actually had coined the term Industrial Revolution. There was a spurt of other neologisms to take into account new social and economic realities: industrialist, engineer, factory, and railway were either entirely new notions or terms that evolved significantly during this period.[1]

Perhaps not the least peculiar aspect of the era was that this particular revolution was effected not by generals, politicians or religious leaders, but by engineers.

This cloddish and often despised class mined the coal, designed the blast furnaces and steam engines, laid out railway lines and flung bridges by the score across rivers and gorges. In sum, they provided the infrastructure on which the new and, it was hoped, universal prosperity was to stand. "These are indeed glorious times for the Engineers," exulted James Nasmyth, the Scottish inventor who designed the first steam hammer.[2]

His euphoric mood was echoed throughout the industrializing world. The engineer of the early industrial age was a pragmatic sort, generally uneducated in the classical sense. But his ability to cope with problems posed by the new technology earned him increasing appreciation. "If we want any work done of an unusual character and send for an architect," Britain's Prince Albert was said to have observed, "he hesitates, debates, trifles; we send for an engineer, and he *does* it." As the century advanced and their profession was put on a more scientific basis, engineers were to realize monumental works with the functional beauty of perfectly resolved equations.[3]

Perhaps inevitably, the importance of their accomplishments was generally underappreciated at the time. Less pardonably, they still are in many cases, despite their historical uniqueness and their contributions to the fund of knowledge of how to get things done.

As James Marston Fitch, professor of architecture at Columbia University, has pointed out, "The 19th century saw three great developments in structural theory: the enclosure of great areas in the Crystal Palace; the spanning of great voids in the Brooklyn Bridge; and the reaching of great heights in the Eiffel Tower. . . . Each of these structures was, in a way, the product of a golden moment of equilibrium, brief in time, special in character, delicate in balance. Their significance was dissipated before men of adequate stature could again appear to grasp it."[4]

Besides being the work of engineers, these three landmark creations had another significant point in common: the imaginative and resourceful use of iron. A banal metal utilized for over 3,000 years for limited production of tools and weapons, iron had always been valued for its hardness and strength. The number of uses it could be put to was limited by the state of technology, however, and local smithies generally were able to satisfy demand from their simple forges until well into the 18th century.

With the coming of the Industrial Revolution, iron's qualities were rediscovered in the light of new needs, and its rapidly growing use virtually transformed the early industrial era into a second Iron Age. If a single development could be pinpointed as the most important in the concatenation of causes that sparked the Industrial Revolution, it might well be the discovery around 1709 by an English iron master, Abraham Darby, that iron could be smelted with coke, made from plentiful coal, rather than with charcoal.

With the help of bigger blast furnaces and more sophisticated metallurgical techniques, iron production made exponential leaps during the 19th century. World output of pig iron, estimated at 1 million tons in 1820, grew to 39.8 million in 1900. Strong as stone in compression but far more resistant to shear and tension, iron freed civil engineers from the arch, the vault, and the dome. For the first time since the 15th-century Italian architect Leon Battista Alberti had formulated the principles of masonry construction, builders could take an entirely new approach—based on intelligent economy rather than sheer mass—to structural problems. The result was what one architectural historian, Carl Condit of the University of Chicago, has called "The most profound and far-reaching revolution in the history of the building arts."[5]

Builders' habits were not always easily changed, however. Paris' central market, Les Halles, was originally conceived in classical masonry in 1851 by Victor Baltard, an assiduous student of Greek and Roman ruins. Emperor Napoleon III, who often had more modern ideas than he has been given credit for, was furious when he saw the structure and had it torn down. Calling in the prefect of Paris, Baron Eugène Haussmann, the emperor decreed that the market should resemble "big umbrellas." Haussmann, who created modern Paris by cutting great swaths—today's boulevards—through the jumbled, still-medieval city, urged Baltard to use iron.

Baltard went back to the drawing board and created the 12 soaring glass and iron pavilions on slim cast-iron columns that caught and delighted the eye from 1867 until they were demolished in 1971. The writer Émile Zola called them the only original monument constructed in France during the 19th century. Later, the architect Mies van der Rohe termed Les Halles "the symbol of the golden age of French building techniques." The end products of those techniques were, among others, the American skyscraper and the Eiffel Tower.

Indeed, there is an intriguing link between the tower and the first true skyscraper, Chicago's Home Insurance Building. Completed in 1885, four years before the Eiffel Tower, the Home Insurance Building was designed with interior iron framing, reducing the walls to nothing more than the protective envelope that characterizes the glass-walled buildings of today.

Its architect, William Le Baron Jenney, drew much of his knowledge of modern iron-framing techniques from his studies in France. Before going to Chicago to become the mentor of many of the brilliant young architects of the Chicago School, such as Louis Sullivan, William Holabird, and Martin Roche, Jenney spent three years in Paris at the École Centrale des Arts et Manufactures, graduating in 1856. Exactly one year after his schoolmate, Gustave Eiffel.[6]

THE IRONY OF Eiffel's career is that the man whom the French proclaim *Le Magicien du Fer* knew very little about metal construction when he graduated from Centrale at age 22. He had in fact studied chemistry, and aspired to nothing more than a job at an uncle's vinegar distillery in his hometown of Dijon, a city known still today for its high-quality vinegar and mustard.

To all appearances a conventional, rather prim, most Victorian young man, Eiffel was disappointed at the turn of family events that upset his comfortable plans to become a maker of fine vinegar. But he gamely took a first job as factotum to the head of a Paris construction firm specializing in railway equipment. The direction of Eiffel's career was thus initially decided by luck.

Although aloof and formal by nature, he appears to have retained a charming modesty until his death at 91. His references to the tower that made him world famous were always marked with mild self-astonishment. But fate was to lend a Sophoclean touch to the life of this basically simple man, dealing Eiffel a blow in a moment of seeming hubris from which he never fully recovered, and which cast an unfortunate and unfair shadow over his reputation in France.

Alexandre Gustave Boenickhausen-Eiffel was the great-great grandson of Jean-René Boenickhausen, who emigrated to France from a village near Cologne in the early 18th century and became a forester. (The builder of the tower was the third of a trio of men of Rhenish origin who shaped the face of Paris in the 19th century. The other two were the engineer Jacques Hittorf, who designed the Champs Elysées and the Place de la Concorde, and Eugène Haussmann.) Jean-René's principal achievement, for our purposes, was to assume the name Eiffel, derived from Germany's Eifel plateau region of his birth, to appear less of a foreigner.

His son Jean-Pierre Henri married the daughter of a prosperous Paris tapestry merchant and became a *maître-tapissier* himself when tapestry making was one of the elite crafts of France. The trade was passed on from father to son for two generations, until Gustave Eiffel's father, François Alexandre, broke the pattern in favor of military adventure by joining Napoleon's Imperial Army at age 16 in 1811. Wounded twice in the Fifth Hussar Regiment during the Italian campaign, he was posted to the garrison at Dijon after Waterloo and there met and married Catherine-Mélanie Moneuse, the daughter of a lumber merchant. The first of three children and only son, Alexandre Gustave was born in Dijon on December 15, 1832.[7]

In his brief memoirs, Gustave Eiffel devotes many pages to a fond description of his childhood in Dijon. Surprisingly for a man of his practical turn of mind, Eiffel, when he was 90, wrote that he remembered those tender years better than any other period of his life. It was an ordinary, happy, provincial childhood, punctuated by occasional raps on the knuckles and Sunday visits to the neighborhood *patisserie*. Good democratic principles were inculcated by Uncle Jean-Baptiste Mollerat, a chemist who had invented a process for distilling vinegar from wood, and who enjoyed locally the reputation of having seen Robespierre guillotined. He frequently reminded the youngster that "all kings are rascals," driving home the point with a stern look through glittering pince-nez that Eiffel never forgot.

Learning was in the traditional French manner, a boring, distasteful, rote process at a prisonlike lycée, and Gustave was an indifferent pupil until his last years there, when two professors awakened his interest in history and literature. He managed the difficult feat of passing a double *baccalauréat* in literature and science, and was sent to the elite Collège Sainte Barbe in Paris to prep for that ambition of all worthy French parents, the prestigious École Polytechnique. Founded in 1795, Polytechnique—imitated in Germany and Belgium, and from Zurich to Vienna and Prague to Saint Petersburg—was largely responsible for France's supremacy in math and science during much of the 19th century.

The capital was a stimulant to the young provincial. Despite the strict Victorian discipline of Sainte Barbe, he found time to discover the joys of the quadrille and to meet his first English girls. "They're very amusing," he wrote home, to the probable consternation of his parents. "Much less reserved than French girls."[8]

Due to a slip during a final exam, Eiffel failed in the summer of 1852 to gain entrance to Polytechnique. His failure to make the cut there seems to have disappointed his family more than Gustave, who never seems to have admitted to grand ambitions or underestimated his real value.

Without missing a beat he opted for the École Centrale des Arts et Manufactures, an institution not the less estimable for lacking Polytechnique's luster. Unlike the state-run, semi-military Polytechnique, whose superbly trained and disciplined graduates usually went on to government service, Centrale was a younger, more liberal private school that graduated solid, self-reliant technicians and engineers.

Eiffel chose chemistry as his major, for he had been given to understand that upon graduation he would have a place at his Uncle Mollerat's vinegar firm in Dijon. But just before he took his degree in 1855, the Eiffel and Mollerat families ceased speaking to each other as the result of a trivial but violent political quarrel. Under the circumstances there was no question of the young graduate's joining his uncle. He rounded up several letters of introduction and began looking for a job in Paris.

As a Centrale graduate he was welcomed by Charles Nepveu, an official in the French Society of Civil Engineers, whose firm made steam engines, rolling stock and other railway equipment. Nepveu offered a salary of $30 per month and the opportunity to learn the business, and Eiffel gladly took the job of personal secretary and man Friday.

The arrangement lasted only a few months, for the high-strung Nepveu was a better engineer than businessman; his company shortly went bankrupt while he had a nervous breakdown. He and his young protégé managed to land on their feet, thanks to a big Belgian railway equipment firm that merged with Nepveu to form the General Railway Equipment Company. Eiffel was made chief of research—with a raise to $50 per month.

Eiffel's providential knock at Nepveu's door put him on the ground floor of the fastest-growing, most dynamic industry of the industrious 19th century. The railway was, literally, the vehicle of the Industrial Revolution. Not only did it provide a reliable, low-cost, high-volume system of land transportation, it also served as an outlet for capital investment, created employment, and stimulated the coal and iron industries. Railway requirements encouraged research into steam power and new approaches to architectural engineering for bridge and train shed construction. For nearly half a century, this was the predominant business of the industrializing world.

After Britain opened the Stockton-Darlington line in 1825, the world's first public railway for freight and passengers, other state railways followed in France in 1828, Germany and Austria in 1835, and the rush was on. During the peak of Britain's "railway mania" in the 1840s, Parliament authorized construction of over 400 railways. France's network was relatively late-blooming, but by the time Gustave Eiffel fortuitously abandoned chemistry for civil engineering, French railway construction was at its peak—nearly 8,000 miles of track were laid from 1852 to 1857—and six main companies had been created.

Eiffel's first big job, at 25, was commissioned by two of those lines, which decided in 1858 to join their networks with a bridge across the Garonne River at Bordeaux. Eiffel was charged with overseeing the whole $600,000 operation and insuring that the June 1860 deadline was met.

Two years was a short time in which to build a 1,600-foot cast-iron railway bridge on six piers across the turbulent Garonne. Eiffel, working 16-hour days, boldly decided to use a time-saving new system of pile driving he had had the occasion to study when he began with Nepveu, but which had never been fully developed. The method, involving hydraulic presses and compressed air to sink the piles, worked as well in the 80-foot-deep river as it had on paper.

The structure opened on time as one of the largest iron bridges of the day, and Eiffel had begun to establish himself as an innovative engineer. He had also set the pattern that was to characterize his projects for the rest of his career: textbook execution of a carefully conceived, theoretically sound plan that freed him from the trial-and-error methods still prevalent in most engineering of the time, especially in Britain and the United States.

At Bordeaux, only one incident appears to have upset Eiffel's precise calculations. A riveter fell into the Garonne one afternoon following a bibulous lunch, and was caught in the current. A strong swimmer who had won a bet when he was 20 by swimming across the Seine at night, Eiffel removed his shoes and ever-present redingote, plunged in and saved the man. "Please be good enough to attach yourselves carefully in the future," he admonished the workers as he decorously buttoned the redingote over his dripping shirt and trousers. When the job was completed, the workers chipped in to have a medal designed showing the bridge and the hydraulic pile driver, and presented it to Eiffel as a token of their esteem.

Master Builder in Iron

His CAREER STARTED, Eiffel began to long for domesticity. It was not satisfactory after all to send his shirts and underclothes to Dijon every week for washing and ironing. "What I need," he wrote his mother, revealing an acute need of modern sensitivity training, "is a good housekeeper who won't get on my nerves too much, who will be as faithful as possible, and who will give me fine children."[1]

He was convinced that Dijon was the only place to find a proper wife, perhaps because of an unhappy affair in Bordeaux that finally required financial consolation for the lady. As it happened, a business associate of Eiffel *père* had a marriageable granddaughter who fit the description and possessed a dowry that met the pretensions of a rising young engineer. Eiffel had actually known Marie Gaudelet since childhood; they were married in 1862, when he was 29, and set up in a comfortable apartment in Paris. They had five children before Marie's untimely death, probably of pneumonia, 15 years later, when she was only 32. Eiffel never remarried.

With the General Railway Equipment Company feeling the effects of a French recession, Eiffel left in 1864 and began free-lancing as a consulting engineer. A job involving delivery of a consignment of locomotives to Egypt gave him the opportunity to visit the recently opened, French-built Suez Canal, then one of the great achievements of engineering. His observations there were to prove useful years later when the builder of Suez, Ferdinand de Lesseps, proposed a similar canal, without locks, across the isthmus of Panama.

By 1867, Eiffel had opened his own metal-working shops in Levallois-Perret, an industrial suburb northwest of Paris, and was awarded a contract to design the iron arch-girders of the machinery hall for the Paris World's Fair of that year. During this machine-proud era, the machinery hall was usually the most important building at a world's fair. Though the hall of 1867 would be surpassed at later fairs, it was the largest until that time, an iron-framed ellipse 1,608 by 1,266 feet, its arches reaching a height of 82 feet above the exhibition floor.

In designing the arches, Eiffel once again eschewed the trial-and-error method of engineering and undertook to determine precisely the elasticity modulus of wrought iron. Drawing on the early scientific studies of Robert Hooke, Thomas Young, and others who had formulated elasticity principles for metals, Eiffel experimented until he had arrived at a workable formula good for all wrought-iron construction.

His published memorandum on the subject took much of the guesswork out of calculating the effects of stress and strain on components of a given iron structure. It constituted an important addition to the small body of scientifically based quantitative calculation available to engineers of the day, many of whom were still relying on theories of structural analysis stemming from the 16th- and 17th-century studies of Palladio and Galileo.

In Eiffel's own career, his formula became one of his most valued tools in creating the sturdy but light structures that became his hallmark, enabling him to reduce trusswork without sacrificing strength and rigidity. The resultant open webbing of his high bridge piers made them invulnerable to the nemesis of hundreds of bridges of the time: wind. Eiffel thus became a precursor of what the American historian, urban planner and architectural critic Lewis Mumford later called "the architecture of the future, light, aerial, open to sunlight, an architecture of voids rather than solids."[2]

Other innovations followed, as Eiffel's company was increasingly invited to bid for the big jobs. Most contracts were for the construction of railway bridges. Although his company handled all forms of metal framework construction, from factories to exhibition halls, train stations to churches, the sudden expansion of railways had ushered in the golden age of bridge building. Longer and higher bridges have been built since the latter half of the 19th century, but it is doubtful that as many have been constructed in a comparable period of time, or that their builders had to grapple with as many unknowns.

Writing their textbooks as they went, engineers independently evolved such tools as submersible pneumatic caissons for laying foundations on the bedrock of river bottoms, steel cable for suspension bridges, and a multiplicity of truss forms. Landmarks of this period included James B. Eads's immense bridge across the Mississippi at Saint Louis, completed in 1874, and the Brooklyn Bridge, built by John and Washington Roebling in 1884, with a record 1,600-foot central span suspended 120 feet above the East River.

Greatest bridge of the century was the tremendous cantilever construction across Scotland's Firth of Forth, opened in 1890. Designed by Sir John Fowler and Benjamin Baker, the Forth railway bridge had two main spans of 1,700 feet each, supported by steel trusswork 330 feet deep. (By comparison, the contemporary Verrazano-Narrows Bridge from Staten Island to Brooklyn has a central span of 4,260 feet.)

Inevitably the new technology took its toll as engineers groped to perfect their methods. Besides fatal falls from high piers and other accidents, workers died of caisson disease, or the bends, while sinking foundations in compressed air chambers. Nor did all deaths occur during construction. With the weight of trains constantly increasing and bridge spans steadily lengthening, railway disasters occurred with alarming frequency—in the United States alone, 251 railway bridges failed in a 10-year period.

Most sensational of the age's accidents was the Tay Bridge disaster in Scotland in 1878. Completed only a year before by Sir Thomas Bouch, the new wrought-iron bridge over the Firth of Tay, near Dundee on the North Sea, was one of the largest and best known of the time. Sir Thomas had badly calculated his wind load factors, however, and a gale was blowing over the firth one December evening as an eight-car train carrying 75 passengers began to cross. Suddenly 13 of the bridge's 85 spans gave way completely. The train and all its passengers were lost.[3]

Not the least of Gustave Eiffel's achievements is that none of his bridges or other structures collapsed, and most are still in use today. Such durability was the result of the sort of creative attention to detail he showed in handling one of his first important contracts as head of his own firm, a bridge across the Sioule River north of Clermont-Ferrand, in France's tortuous Massif Central. Completed in 1869, the structure's 820-foot deck stood 262 feet above the river, making it one of the highest bridges in the world at the time, and a direct technological ancestor of the Eiffel Tower.[4]

The Sioule Bridge incorporated three innovations for Eiffel. First, while retaining cast iron for the vertical edges of his hollow, four-sided piers, he abandoned the heavy, brittle metal for the first time in favor of wrought iron—lighter and more elastic under wind loads—for the trusswork. Then he incurved the edges of the piers to give them increased footing and greater stability at the base. Finally, he developed a new method of "launching" the bridge's decks, using a system of rollers on rockers, which supported the deck evenly as it was pushed straight out over the chasm to meet the next pier. All three of these Eiffelian traits—preference for wrought iron, careful attention to wind bracing, and a novel method of erection—are to be found in evolved form in the thousand-foot tower.

In the following years, Eiffel and Company constructed 42 railway bridges and viaducts for French lines. It also began to bid in international competition for projects abroad.

The Portuguese national railways chose him in 1875 for the delicate task of putting a bridge across the Douro River at Oporto. The great depth of the Douro prohibited the use of a central pier, meaning that its 525-foot width would have to be spanned by other means. In the United States, the solution would likely have been a suspension bridge similar to that which John Roebling put over the Niagara in 1855. But in Europe engineers were leery of suspension bridges. Too many had failed, sometimes simply because marching men or herds of cattle accidentally struck a resonant frequency that set the bridges oscillating.

Eiffel therefore designed a trussed parabolic arch to support the central span, and set the arch's sides at oblique angles to each other to give it extra wind resistance. Launching the arch, the largest ever attempted until then, was another problem, since supporting scaffolding could not be erected in the river.

The Oporto bridge after completion in 1876.

Eiffel's ingenious solution was to build the two halves of the arch out toward each other, supporting them from above with steel cables attached to piers on the banks. As work progressed, more cables were added to the gradually lengthening sections until the two halves joined like giant metal mandibles 200 feet above the center of the Douro. Completed in 1876, the magnificent bridge was christened the Maria Pia in honor of the queen of Portugal.

Eiffel's triumph over the Douro led a French railway company operating in the Massif Central to contemplate a bridge at the record height of 400 feet over the rushing Truyère River at Garabit. Such a bridge would save 12 miles of track—if it could be built. Eiffel responded with plans for a bridge similar to the Maria Pia, but on a far grander scale: a height of 400 feet, a length of 1,850 feet, with the deck supported by five trusswork metal piers and a great parabolic arch with a 541-foot chord. It would be the highest arched bridge in the world, the equivalent, Gustave Eiffel liked to point out, of standing Paris' Vendôme column atop the spires of Notre Dame Cathedral. Garabit would be acclaimed as "one of the victories of modern engineering." It was Eiffel's masterpiece until his thousand-foot tower a decade later.[5]

An undertaking of that size in France, with its ultra-centralized government, had to have the authorization of the Ministry of Bridges and Roads. After examining the project, the ministry gave its approval in June 1879, prudently stating that Eiffel's successful completion of a similar bridge over the Douro gave him a reasonable chance at Garabit, and acknowledging that "Monsieur Eiffel is the only person with such experience, since it is he who invented the means of stiffening piers and bridge deck against wind action."

Eiffel went to work in his usual methodical fashion, basing everything on meticulous computations. Stress in the trusses, for example, was to be limited to exactly 13 pounds per square millimeter under the combined action of train loads and wind, giving a cross-section of the members 50 percent greater than if wind had been neglected as a load factor. He studied the effect of temperature changes on the metal components and found that pressure at the crown of the arch varied by only 1.39 pounds per square millimeter during a change of 30 degrees centigrade.

Leaving nothing to chance, especially where wind was concerned, Eiffel factored in lateral pressure on the bridge deck with and without a train crossing it, going so far as to take into account exactly what percentage of the train's surface would be sheltered from wind by the deck's girders. He also fixed in advance the exact speed at which train traffic would have to be suspended. The Tay Bridge disaster would not be repeated at Garabit.

When the moment came to launch the tremendous arch, Eiffel proceeded much as he had at Oporto. Once the iron piers on either side of the Truyère River had been raised, steel cables were fastened to them and dropped to the halves of the arch being built

Construction of the bridge at Garabit in 1883, with its arches 400 feet above the Truyère River. (Photo RMN)

out from the bases of the piers. As more girders were riveted into place and the halves lengthened, additional cables were attached to outer extremities, hanging them securely above the gorge. The breaking point of each cable was 85 tons, whereas during erection no cable actually bore more than 15 tons.

The job took slightly less than five years. When the proof load, consisting of a 75-ton locomotive pulling 22 cars each weighing 15 tons, moved ponderously across the Garabit Viaduct in November 1884, the loaded arch had a deflection of eight millimeters—precisely what Eiffel had calculated.

By the 1880s, the would-be vinegar maker from Dijon had become one of the world's master builders, working in the very forefront of the technology of the age. The number and diversity of his company's projects from 1867 to 1885 is astounding by any measure. They included:

- The Viana Bridge, Portugal. A combined road and railway bridge completed in 1877, the 2,414-foot Viana was built on nine masonry piers sunk by Eiffel's compressed air method. The deck, weighing 1,764 tons, was built entirely onshore and launched in one piece. It was the largest bridge deck ever to be so launched.

- The Pest train station, Hungary. A vast, ornate structure enclosing 140,000 square feet, the Pest station was also completed in 1877. It was one of the first examples of the combined metal and masonry architecture that would become Art Nouveau, the main decoration being the exposed metal components themselves.

- The Tan An Bridge, Cochin China (now Vietnam). One of Eiffel's many bridges in French Indochina, the Tan An, completed in 1880, involved launching a clear span 262 feet across a deep, swift-running river, which made supporting scaffolding impossible. Eiffel divided the deck into two sections and pushed them toward each other in overhang until they met above the river and were joined. He used for the first time this "bootstrap" method that would let him put bridges across rivers and gorges that would otherwise have been impossible to span.

- Dome of the Nice Observatory. Eiffel built the iron trusswork and exterior of Charles Garnier's 74-foot-diameter observatory dome in 1885, the largest of its day. He added an original feature: the rotating dome was not on conventional rollers but on a frictionless floating ring that permitted easy turning of the 110-ton dome by hand.

- Prefabricated campaign bridges. Designed for the army, these portable bridges were composed of a small number of standardized elements that could be assembled rapidly by non-specialized workers but were sturdy enough to support the passage of heavy artillery. Widely used by the French Army in Indochina, they were adopted by the Russian, Austro-Hungarian, and Italian armies.

The list of Eiffel's innovative, iron-based projects could go on, including covered markets, gasworks, iron framing for the church of Notre Dame des Champs in Paris, the city's Bon Marché—the world's first department store—and Galliéra Museum, buildings for the Paris World's Fair of 1878, and still more train stations and bridges in Europe, South America and Indochina.

But the most important of his structures yet unmentioned is universally known not for its usefulness but, like the thousand-foot tower, its symbolism. Perhaps appropriately, this thoroughly practical man was either to create or to be instrumental in building the two best-known national symbols of the practical-minded modern world: the Eiffel Tower and the Statue of Liberty.

"Liberty Enlightening the World" was of course the work of Frédéric August Bartholdi—except that once the Alsatian sculptor had designed his plaster model of the feminine figure with raised torch and spiked crown, he was at a loss as to how to translate it into the colossus intended to symbolize Franco-American friendship.

The figure was to be 151 feet tall, by far the greatest statue ever raised, with a head 17 feet from chin to cranium, an index finger eight feet long, and an extended right arm 42 feet long and 12 feet thick. "Liberty" would dwarf the fabled statues of antiquity, whether Egypt's 66-foot-high Sphinx of Giza, Greece's 40-foot Olympian Zeus and 100 foot Colossus of Rhodes, or Japan's 40-foot Great Buddha in Kamakura. But Bartholdi was uncertain what sort of construction would enable a statue of such size to be transported across the North Atlantic, set up on Bedloe Island, and then bear its own weight and withstand the winds of Upper New York Bay. Masonry was out of the question.[6]

Bartholdi took the problem to Eiffel in 1881. The engineer whose career had been spent finding ways to subtract superfluous mass from enormous structures—proving that less is more somewhat before Mies van der Rohe got credit for the idea—designed an iron skeleton for a *hollow* statue. The surface would be sheets of metal attached to an interior framework. Bartholdi first tried bronze for the exterior, but switched to copper sheets $\frac{3}{32}$ of an inch thick when bronze proved too heavy.

Eiffel designed a skeleton resting on vertical steel beams planted in the statue's granite pedestal. The hardest technical problem was posed by the torch-bearing arm, which is in an inherently weak overhang position. Eiffel solved that by running the arm's supporting beams on through the body and across to the extreme left side, counterbalancing the overhang. The frame weighed only 162,000 pounds, compared to nearly 200,000 pounds for the hammered copper sheets of the exterior.

The long, frustrating process that had begun in 1875 when a French historian, Edouard René Lefebvre de Laboulaye, had formed the Franco-American Union to sponsor the statue as a gift to the United States at the Philadelphia Centennial Exposition of 1876, was finally bearing fruit. Difficulty in raising the $400,000 from private citizens to finance the project had caused Bartholdi to fall far behind the initial delivery date of 1876, though part of the statue, the upraised torch, was displayed at Philadelphia. But by spring of 1883 the skeleton was standing in the work yards of Gaget, Gauthier & Company near Rue de Chazelles in Paris.

For over a year, bemused Parisians watched the statue take shape behind its wooden scaffolding as workmen hung the 300-odd copper sheets on Eiffel's framework. Strange to tell today, the site was often used as a soapbox by French citizens who made impromptu speeches praising the United States of America and the way it was defining and practicing freedom. The French government, which had remained aloof from the project during the fund-raising phase, now began to see it as a gesture that would gain useful good will for the shaky Third Republic—and incidentally combat the country's incipient monarchism by emphasizing democratic principles. It therefore offered the services of the French Navy in transporting the statue across the Atlantic.

After "Liberty" was officially presented to the United States in a ceremony in Paris on July 4, 1884, the statue was dismantled, its metal components numbered for reference and packed in 85 wooden cases, and sent to the port of Rouen farther down the Seine. There the cases were loaded onto the three-masted French warship *Isère*, which arrived in New York in October 1885 to a cacophony of blaring tugboats and cheering if huddled masses.

Interior bracing of the Statue of Liberty, 1881. Message signed Bartholdi reads,
"Praise to M. Eiffel with thanks from the Statue of Liberty who owes him her iron skeleton."
(Collection Tour Eiffel)

GUSTAVE EIFFEL, an engineer living the "glorious times" of his profession, was at the peak of his career. Contemporary photographs show him at 55 to have been small but well proportioned, with large, thickish hands, close-cropped, graying beard and hair, and heavy-lidded light blue eyes. If anything was remarkable about his appearance it was his serene, hooded gaze, which gave him a look of complete self-possession free of interior conflict of any sort: dull company, perhaps, but you would feel safe crossing one of his bridges.

Professionally, Eiffel had a self-confident mastery that led him to disdain secrecy. He routinely published the blueprints and calculations of his projects once they were completed. He was an engineer through and through, scorning superfluous embellishments. When exasperated by a bad design, he was often heard to mutter, "Stupid as an architect." In the rapidity and sureness with which he overcame technical problems, he appears to fit poet Paul Valéry's description of the great builders of the age, who "conceived their structures visibly as a complete whole, rather than in two mental phases, one relating to form and the other to matter . . . they *thought* in materials."[7]

The one thing Eiffel lacked on the eve of the 1889 Paris World's Fair was fame, for he remained relatively unknown outside engineering circles. And it may be true, as the internationally famous Swiss architect and city planner Charles-Edouard Jeanneret, better known as Le Corbusier, has suggested, that "He was pained by not being seen as a creator of beauty . . . His calculations were always inspired by an admirable instinct for proportion, his goal was elegance."[8]

The thousand-foot tower he had proposed for the Exposition would make his name a household word in many lands. It would even be considered beautiful by some. And whatever the tallest tower would come to mean to the generations who lived in its lanky shadow or who traveled far to see it, it gave a neat dramatic structure to the life of Gustave Eiffel. For it was not only his greatest metal structure, it was also his last.

The Tower Rises

IT WOULD BE HARD to find a less martial terrain than the Champ de Mars. Located in the quietly residential 7th Arrondissement, bordered by some of the most prized real estate in Paris, it is a favorite park of chic *mamans* who wheel expensive English prams beneath its double rows of plane trees. Nearby, children wearing outfits from the likes of Baby Dior try for brass rings on the hand-cranked merry-go-round. There is not a uniform in sight, except for a bronze Marshal Joffre on horseback forever urging his troops to stand on the Marne, and a handful of park police quick to blow the whistle on toddlers or tourists who dare set foot on the manicured grass. The only armada is sailed in two small sparkling pools; the only shouts emanate from the excited young audience at a puppet show.

To be sure, the Champ de Mars has occasionally witnessed history. Louis XV founded the Royal Military School there and transformed the sandy plain into a parade ground where he could pass in review 10,000 men in battle formation arrayed from one end to the other. Hardy 18th-century French aviators found the area ideal for experiments in their hot-air Montgolfiers. After the Revolution, secular holidays such as the Feast of the Federation were celebrated on the Champ de Mars, with Tallyrand saying Mass at a gigantic altar set in the middle of the field. When the Terror reigned, the mayor of Paris was guillotined there.

A triumphant Napoleon Bonaparte, a graduate of the École Militaire ("Should make an excellent naval officer," a perceptive military mind noted on Bonaparte's application form when he entered), distributed the imperial standards to his victorious troops there in 1804. Thereafter, the area's military vocation declined, seemingly paralleling the fate of French arms. Horse races were its main activity during the Second Empire, until the Longchamp track was created in 1855. During the great period of world's fairs, the Champ de Mars was the site of the Paris fairs of 1867, 1878, and of course 1889, as well as later ones in 1900 and 1937.

BENEATH THE SURFACE, the Champ de Mars is much like the rest of Paris: gray plastic clay about 50 feet deep resting on a solid foundation of chalk. Its proximity to the Seine, however, has left it with an upper layer 20 feet thick of compact sand and gravel which slopes away toward the river. The closer to the Seine, the less stable the area's geological character, as Gustave Eiffel found when he received initial results of bore samplings of the tower site in early January 1887. In view of administrative complications, this threatened to be the first obstacle to his tower.[1]

Except for a narrow band beside the Seine, which was the property of the City of Paris, the Champ de Mars belonged to the state. Negotiations with the government for a 20-year lease of land for the tower would be long and drawn-out, and the one thing Eiffel did not have now was time. He could have immediate authorization from the city to build the tower on its land, but the samples raised questions about the stability of substrata there. Eiffel would have no problem with the tower's east and south feet—the tower's four feet correspond exactly to the cardinal points of the compass—since they were far enough from the Seine to be on firm ground.

The north and west feet, however, would have to rest close beside the river, where the upper stratum was composed of soft alluvial deposits of sandy mud and clay mixed with detritus such as logs, pottery fragments, bones of domestic animals eons dead, and masonry pieces from a long-buried wall. This would not do for foundations, and it remained to be seen at what depths the substrata became firm enough to support the tower. The soundings Eiffel had ordered from a subcontractor were inconclusive on this point, so he decided to conduct his own study.

Using cylindrical pneumatic caissons seven feet in diameter, he dug to a depth of 48 feet. Workmen in the caissons turned up layers of sandy clay and fine sand above compact gravel which, if solidly based, could support foundations. To be certain, Eiffel bored five feet more and hit what he was looking for: the good gray clay of Paris. By sinking the foundations for the Seine-side piers 16 feet deeper than the other two, he would have solid footing for a thousand-foot tower weighing an estimated 10,600 tons, including heavy masonry bases under each foot.

Work began on all four foundations. They did not have to go extremely deep, but since they were at or below the level of the Seine, excavation would be hampered by water seepage unless pneumatic caissons were used. Eiffel had had considerable experience with caissons in sinking his bridge foundations. On March 26, his shops began building 16 iron caissons, four for each pier.

Measuring 50 feet long, 20 feet wide and 10 feet deep, each caisson had a work chamber six feet high within which several men could wield shovels and pickaxes. They entered from the top through an air lock, and pressure was kept high enough to repel below-surface water. The walls of the 34-ton caissons were wedge-shaped at the bottom to form cutting edges, making the iron boxes sink as earth was hoisted out in buckets through airtight hatches. The interiors were illuminated by electricity, something of a luxury since electric lighting was just then being introduced in Paris homes.

Work went rapidly—there were no cases of the bends, thanks to strict application of rules governing the rate of decompression when the men left the caissons—and when 40,500 cubic yards of earth had been removed from the four sites, the foundations themselves were laid. Each pier would rest on a massive pile of cement and stone set obliquely in the earth so that the curving columns that bore the tower's weight would exert their thrust at right angles to the mass.

Into each excavation was poured a bed of quick-setting cement 20 feet deep to serve as a nonsettling base for the masonry. Over the cement, Eiffel placed enormous blocks of limestone quarried

Cutaway view of the caissons in operation, with air lock at top and work chamber below.
(Collection Tour Eiffel)

in central France, an area known for its solid travertine stone. The limestone in turn was capped by two layers of ultra-hard cut stone from Château Landon, the quarry that had provided the stone for the Arch of Triumph and the Sacré Coeur Basilica.

Embedded in the center of each mass were two great anchor bolts 26 feet long and four inches in diameter, to which a cylindrical flanged iron shoe was attached; the column would be bolted to the shoe and thus locked into the heart of the stone mass. Pressure from the columns was to be 10.2 pounds per square inch, whereas the stone could support 421 pounds per square inch — 41 times the expected load. Additional excess safety was provided by the anchor bolts, which were not actually necessary to keep the tower from overturning. Theoretically it would be kept stable by its own weight.

Thus far, the tower's foundations were examples of classical civil engineering. The thoroughness and speed with which they were laid — they were in place on June 30, five months after the first spadeful of earth had been turned — were typical of Eiffel, but they involved no particular innovation. Where his innate inventiveness came into play, however, was in the design of the cylindrical shoes that would receive the columns.

In the hollow of each shoe Eiffel placed a piston that could be moved by water under pressure. This was a truly brilliant stroke, for these hydraulic jacks gave him the ability to raise or lower each of the 16 columns to insure that the piers were in a perfectly horizontal plane when the time came to join them with a band of girders at the first platform. If the piers, in their separate rise, were even infinitesimally out of plane, the deviation would throw the tower disastrously off vertical when it reached its full height. With the jacks, each capable of lifting 900 tons, Eiffel would be able to fine-tune the ungainly assemblage into perfect alignment.

Eiffel's calculations indicated that pressure on the earth beneath the masonry foundations would range from a minimum of 58 pounds to a maximum of 64 pounds per square inch, depending on wind force and which pier was being considered. This was well within the limits that the substrata could bear. In fact, it is not much more pressure than a well-fed gentleman exerts on the floor when sitting on a spindly-legged chair.

The tower's relative lightness is one of the most astonishing things about it. As he had at the Douro and at Garabit, Eiffel reduced metalwork to the absolute minimum consistent with security; there was not an inch of superfluous trussing. To illustrate: if the tower's iron girders and braces were melted down and spread out into a square sheet equal in area to the four acres enclosed by its base, the sheet would be a mere two-and-a-half inches thick. And if an imaginary cylinder is conjured up with the tower's dimensions, that is, with a diameter equal to its base and a height of 1,000 feet, the air in the cylinder would weigh nearly 10,000 tons—compared with the tower's 8,000 tons of iron.

WELL BEFORE the first girder had been raised or rivet placed, Eiffel was certain of the tower's exact weight. He could guarantee that the combined forces of gravity and wind, pulling and tearing year round at his lacy lattice, would not crumple it at some unpredictable moment of stress. But he was working without such fundamental tools of modern engineering as computers and systems engineering methods. Moreover, he was advancing into an uncharted area of technology.

The "one exceptional way in which the project differed from works of earlier periods as well as from contemporary ones" was once described by Robert M. Vogel, curator of mechanical and civil engineering at the Smithsonian Institution in Washington, D.C. He explained Eiffel's audacious leap into the technical unknown by observing that:

> In almost every case, these other works had evolved, in a natural and progressive way, from a fundamental concept firmly based upon precedent. This was true of such notable structures of the time as the Brooklyn Bridge and, to a lesser extent, the Forth Bridge. For the design of his tower, there was virtually no experience in structural history from which Eiffel could draw other than a series of high piers that his own firm had designed earlier for railway bridges.[2]

And none of Eiffel's previous piers had reached even half as high as he now intended to go.

Once again, he put his faith in figures and detailed planning. Soon after Maurice Koechlin and Emile Nougier had presented their initial plan of the tower in 1884, he had his draftsmen turn out blueprints for every piece of metal to be used in it: 5,329 mechanical drawings representing 18,038 separate items. These drawings alone took 30 draftsmen 18 months to produce and covered 14,352 square feet of paper.

Eiffel's greatest difficulty derived from the tower's odd angles. If it had been only an "assemblage of iron ladders," a few basic elements could have been designed and then copied thousands of times, as they had been for Eiffel's portable bridges. But the tower's curved, weight-bearing edges describe irregular arcs and the trussing of its 28 panels varies gradually from bottom to top.

Each piece therefore had to be designed separately, taking into account the variable inclination of columns and braces along every foot of the tower's height. In addition, every rivet hole had to be drawn in at precisely the right spot, so that all the on-site workers would have to do was to place one-third of the 2.5 million rivets, the rest being placed at the shops in advance. The Eiffel Tower was one of the first examples of large-scale industrialized construction; all calculations had to be accurate to one-tenth of a millimeter.

When it came to determining the strength of the tower, Eiffel paradoxically ignored the weight of visitors, despite the fact that the structure was designed to accommodate a maximum of 10,416 persons at once on its three platforms. Their total weight, he figured, at an average of 154 pounds, would be 800 tons, or less than 10 percent of the tower's total weight. "The violence of the wind that we estimated in determining the tower's strength," Eiffel explained later, "was so great that it would make visiting impossible. Besides, the visitors' weight produced negligible stress compared with that created by the weight of the tower itself and high winds."

The real problem was the wind. Eiffel knew his old enemy well and had outsmarted it in every one of his tall bridge piers.

In designing the tower, he adopted two extreme hypotheses to simulate wind force. In the first, he took into account a wind of 134 miles per hour exerted evenly over the tower's entire surface from top to bottom; in the second, a wind of 148 miles per hour at the top, diminishing gradually to 105 miles per hour at the bottom. Never had such winds been observed in Paris. In addition, the surface to be struck was deliberately exaggerated. The upper half of the structure was assumed to be a solid surface taking the wind full-face; the intermediate area, where the open spaces are much greater, was figured to be four times its actual surface; below that, the four piers were assumed to be solid surfaces rather than open trusses.

Then coefficients for vertical weight and wind force were combined to give a total working coefficient for the entire tower and each of its 28 trusswork panels. The figures showed that the mathematical center of the wind's action in the first hypothesis would be at a height of 278 feet, and in the second, 323 feet. The wind's total force, or overturning moment, was then compared with the tower's predetermined resistance to overturning, or moment of stability, considering its weight, height, and base area. The moment of stability was greater. (In reality, the tower would sway only about 4¾ inches in a strong wind; due to dilatation of its iron, on a sunny day the top slowly describes an ellipse of seven inches as the sun strikes it at different angles.)

The tower would stand because of Eiffel's grasp of a paradox: victory over wind is achieved not through an accumulation of brute force, buy by reducing the supporting elements of an openwork structure until the wind has virtually nothing to seize. In other words, the Eiffel Tower's real strength is in its voids as much as in its iron.

ON JULY 1, 1887, the tower began to rise. The jagged stumps of its four colossal box piers, inclined toward the center of the base area at an angle of 54 degrees, seemed to reach a little farther toward each other every day. Finished iron pieces arrived regularly by

A pier begins to rise, July 1887.

horse-drawn drays from Eiffel's shops in Levallois-Perret, about three miles away. During construction his shops would turn out up to 400 tons of girders and trusses per month.

The pieces were hoisted into position by tall, steam-powered cranes. Eiffel deliberately used girders weighing no more than three tons, a relatively light maximum weight in view of the size of the structure. He had learned that using small components was faster and safer, even if this method did require more riveting, for cranes could be smaller and more mobile. The chances of accidents were reduced, and if one did occur the consequences were less serious. Using bigger girders would have slowed the entire operation and required more expensive and complicated construction methods.

As it was, Eiffel's team of experienced workmen—most had been with him at Garabit, some even before—erected the tower piers with assembly-line speed. First they placed temporary pins in joints, then replaced these with bolts and finally rivets as related pieces moved into position. Of the tower's total of 2,500,000 rivets, nearly 60 percent were placed in the shops, meaning that much less time-consuming on-site work. Thus the crew could be kept small for such a project, numbering only 121 on the site. It was supervised by one of Eiffel's most trusted veterans, Jean Compagnon. Fifty years old, Compagnon had joined Eiffel and Company in 1876, and was foreman on all its important jobs, including the Maria Pia and Garabit.

When the columns began to approach the tops of the cranes, Eiffel shifted to an ingenious system of creeper cranes inside the piers themselves. Mounted on the inclined tracks that would later be used by the tower's elevators, the 13-ton cranes could pivot 360 degrees and be moved up the tracks periodically to follow construction as it progressed. They were the heart of Eiffel's system at this stage and greatly impressed visitors to the site, such as the newspaper reporter who came away to write: "It is curious and interesting to watch these four lifting machines climbing ever higher along with the iron columns. They turn left, right, in, out, picking up the huge metal beams and placing them exactly where they are supposed to go."[3]

As the columns rose, the moment drew nearer when their inclination would topple them unless they were given support. Eiffel's calculations predicted that this would happen—in technical terms, their centers of gravity would be located outside the area on which their bases rested—at a height of 92 feet. The columns were not to be joined until they reached the level of the first platform at 180 feet, so temporary bracing was needed.

Twelve wooden, derrick-like pylons 90 feet tall were built and placed beneath the three interior columns of each pier. These were the first of two major scaffoldings required during the tower's construction. The other, begun shortly after the 12 pylons were in place, was composed of four platforms, each 150 feet high and 82 feet long, one in the center of every face of the tower. They were joined to form a square frame that would bear the increasing inward pressure of the piers as they rose above the 90-foot pylons; the frame also supported the heavy iron girders and trusswork when they were raised to unite the piers permanently.

Diagram of 90-foot wooden pylons that supported rising piers. Sand-filled metal cylinders for final adjustment of pier can be seen atop each pylon.

The 12 pylons would have been no more than ordinary false-work had not Eiffel incorporated on their top platforms an adroit complement to the hydraulic jacks at the bases of the columns. This second system to be used in adjusting the piers' angle was simplicity itself: sand-filled metal cylinders resting on the platforms and attached to the columns, accompanied by another set of hydraulic jacks. The cylinders were fitted with pistons at the top and plugs at the bottom. The columns leaned against the pistons. If a column was too high by even a fraction of an inch, the plug could be pulled and fine sand allowed to run out until the piston—and the column—was lowered to the correct position. If a column was too low, the jack beside the cylinder could push the column back to the proper angle. If simplicity of conception and economy of means are signs of genius, touches like these defined Eiffel.

THE TRUNCATED PIERS reached 92 feet on October 10 and began leaning, imperceptibly, against the wooden pylons. Ten tons of iron had been mounted with 98,000 rivets.

Somewhat before then it had become apparent even to the most skeptical Parisian that the foolish structure might really be built, or at least that the attempt would continue until it ended in disaster. The latter eventuality was very much in the minds of some, particularly a number of solid citizens who lived near the Champ de Mars. It took little imagination to envision the gangling metal monster toppling onto nearby residences. One nervous gentleman was sufficiently shaken by the prospect to bring suit against the City of Paris to stop construction. Work came to a halt.[4]

Time, whose wingèd chariot had harried Eiffel ever since the Exposition committee had dawdled for months over its decision, threatened to overrun him unless the suit could be resolved quickly. The city fathers had confidence in Eiffel—up to a point. But they refused to accept responsibility for damage to persons or property caused by the thousand-foot tower. The buck stopped at Eiffel, who, having already put up most of the money for the project, now agreed to undertake construction at his own risk and to be financially responsible for any accidents. If the tower proved dangerous, he would be charged with its demolition.

Following the artists' protest, this second brouhaha over the tower was the last concerted effort to stop its construction, but it would be a long time before all doubt and concern were laid to rest. One French math professor predicted flatly that if the structure ever reached the height of 748 feet, it would ineluctably collapse. As the tower's shadow lengthened, many people peered intently at it on sunny days, watching for signs of wavering. Lightning and electricity were little understood by the popular mind, and some feared that burying conduits from the tower's lightning rods in the bed of the Seine would kill fish.

Then as now, the media eagerly fanned the flames of controversy. James Gordon Bennett's Paris edition of the New York *Herald* found the tower an easy target, sneering at "the modern Tower of Babel" and reporting that it had changed the city's electrical conditions. "The frequency of heavy storms which do not clear the air is taken by many to bear out this theory," the paper explained with a straight face. "People who have watched the tower closely and attentively have remarked the large quantities of heavy rain and thunder clouds which gather round it and then, as if deprived by the lightning conductors of part of their electricity, are blown farther on and break in showers far away in quite another part of town."

A popular Paris daily, *Le Matin*, headlined a scare story in early 1888, "The Tower is Sinking!" "If it has really begun to sink," the paper editorialized, "any further building should stop and sections already built should be demolished as quickly as possible."[5]

Exactly the opposite was true, of course. The tower was rising so fast that Parisians could hardly believe their eyes. Its growth was compared to the steady, organic development of a tree, imperceptible during a brief visit but constant and persistent. Due to Eiffel's meticulous planning, the prefabrication of most pieces, and the relatively small work force, there was little of the clamor usually associated with huge construction projects.

A newspaper reporter, apparently also part poet, visited the tower during these early months and gave this impression of the site:

> I was standing at a height of about 200 feet, among a maze of ironwork painted with red lead, drilled with holes and arranged in crisscross fashion as far as the eye could see. Above a confused grayish mass of timber, and looking very small in such a gigantic setting, 250 workmen came and went in a perfectly orderly way, carrying long beams on their shoulders, climbing up and down through the latticed ironwork with surprising agility. The rapid hammer blows of the riveters could be heard, and they worked with fires that burned with the clear trembling flame of will-o'-the-wisps. The four cranes, one for each pillar, which brought up the pieces for this vast metallic framework one by one, stood out

Workers descending from their riveting platform. (Collection Tour Eiffel)

against the sky with their great arms. During short winter days, when night falls the 20 rivet forges blaze in the high wind, casting a sinister glow over this tangle of girders until it has a fantastic appearance. The men work as late as possible and move about like shadows between these dark red smoky fires.[6]

The smoothness of Eiffel's construction techniques contrasted sharply with the other great engineering project of the day, Benjamin Baker's Forth Bridge, over Scotland's River Forth estuary, then going up. As with most British and American civil engineering projects, workers at the site received the elements of the colossal cantilever bridge, for several years the world's longest span, in a semi-finished state. They then had to consult blueprints and put the finishing touches to metal beams and trusses, shaping and drilling them to specification on the spot.

The two projects were quite different, but it is safe to say that the thousand-foot tower would never have been ready for the 1889 World's Fair if not for Eiffel's prefabrication techniques. His 20 riveting teams had only to line up the tower's pre-punched holes and drive their glowing rivets home—in all, an average of 1,650 rivets per working day. Eiffel was well on his way to setting, as one architectural historian later observed, "new world standards in the design and erection of very tall structures."

The quadrangular piers were now nearing the height of 180 feet—one of the most critical moments. At this level, they would be joined by an iron belt of horizontal trussing running from pier to pier. Twenty-five feet deep, the trussing would form the top of a pedestal with the piers as legs. On this the rest of the tower—another 800 feet of it—would sit. The trussing thus had to be rigid enough to unite the leaning piers into a solid base and also be perfectly horizontal.

The question was whether the 16 columns of the four piers would meet the belt at precisely the right height and at exactly the predetermined spots where the rivet holes had been bored. During their rise, engineers with measured lengths of steel wire frequently checked the positions of the piers. Still, it was the first time Eiffel or any other engineer had attempted to maneuver iron piers weighing 440 tons, with dimensions roughly equal to the twin towers of Notre Dame Cathedral, within tolerances of only a few inches. When the piers were completed in early December, the girders of the trusswork were raised to the top of the four 150-foot platforms and riveted together. Then began the painstaking, infinitely delicate process of joining the massive iron frame to the piers.

This was the moment Eiffel had foreseen when he installed hydraulic jacks in the base shoe of each column and had positioned sand-filled cylinders atop the 90-foot pylons. Moreover, during erection of the piers he had deliberately kept the columns slightly closer to the vertical than their final angle would be, so that ultimate corrections could be made by lowering rather than by raising them. As if he were adjusting a gigantic precision instrument—though with vastly more primitive means than those available to today's engineers—Eiffel slowly brought the 16 columns into line, slightly nudging one with a jack, minutely lowering another by releasing a small quantity of sand from a cylinder.

When each column reached the proper height and angle, workmen drove iron wedges beneath it to fix it in place. So well did the system work that only three or four men could align each tremendous pier; so well had the foundations been laid and the piers mounted that in no instance did more than 2½ inches separate the outreaching beams from the horizontal frame.

On March 26, 1888, the operation was completed, without so much as a file or hand-drill being used to correct the alignment of the rivet holes. With barely more than one year remaining before the structure was due to open, many Parisians thought the tower looked more like a hulking metal beast crouched on all fours than the tall, graceful tower Eiffel had promised. But he himself could breathe a sigh of relief. As he wrote later, "Joined by the belt of girders, the piers formed a solid table with a wide base. The sight of it alone was enough to brush aside any fear of its overturning. We no longer had to worry about a major accident, and any minor ones that might occur now could not compromise completion of the structure."[7]

Fine-tuning one of the 16 columns, March 1888. Workers at left operated pump to force water into hollow shoe at base of column. When adjustment was completed, worker at right drove iron wedges into place. (Collection Tour Eiffel)

EIFFEL'S CONFIDENCE at this point, in the success of his tower and in himself was total. It may then have been an understandable excess of pride that led him to assume responsibility for still another project, even as the tower reached only the halfway mark. Vaster and still more daring than the tower, this task similarly promised to realize an old dream through methodical application of new technology.

A canal through the isthmus of Central America had fired imaginations since the day in 1513 when Balboa discovered that only about 50 miles of land separated the Atlantic from the Pacific in this part of the New World. In 1525, Hernando Cortez drew up a plan for joining the two oceans, and thereafter many maritime nations probed that narrow but intractable neck of jungle, swamp, mountain and river.

Explorers repeatedly searched for the passage that would save up to 2,000 miles on the voyage from Europe to the Pacific, and cut nearly 8,000 miles from the Cape Horn route from the East to the West coasts of the United States. France and Holland, Britain and the United States surveyed the area, signed treaties with Colombia and Nicaragua, which controlled the isthmus, and fought diplomatic duels with each other over it. The first transportation link between Atlantic and Pacific came in 1855, when the United States completed a railway across Panama.

Projects for the canal became a standard subject at international geographical conferences in Europe, such as the ones in Antwerp in 1871 and in Paris in 1879. The latter meeting, the International Interoceanic Canal Study Conference, was presented with some 50 plans for canals—across Nicaragua, across Panama, with locks, at sea level.[8]

The meeting was dominated by the impressive, white-maned figure of Ferdinand de Lesseps, whose Suez Canal had opened in 1869. Now a vigorous 75—10 years previously he had married an 18-year-old Creole girl by whom he sired nine children—Lesseps had been dubbed a *Grand Français* by his countrymen as a result of his having built the Suez, and enjoyed immense prestige in academic, financial and political circles. A diplomat by profession rather than an engineer, he appears to have seen a Panama canal as the climax of his career, despite efforts by his son Charles to dissuade him. Also, he insisted at the Paris conference that a sea-level canal, without locks, would work in Panama just as it had at Suez.

After two weeks of debate, the 135 engineers, businessmen, geographers and entrepreneurs attending the conference voted on May 29 in favor of the sea-level plan. Only eight conferees opposed the idea, maintaining that a system of locks would be needed to negotiate such natural obstacles as the 400-foot-high Culebra range and the torrential Chagres River. One of the main figures of this minority was Gustave Eiffel.

Lesseps was named president of the Panama Interoceanic Canal Company and began raising capital. He traveled as far as New York to promote the venture, stopping off to look over the Brooklyn Bridge then being built, and speaking before the American Society of Civil Engineers. In France, the company's experts evaluated the costs of excavation and construction at $214 million. But Lesseps started out with the barely $6 million that came in mainly from small French investors impressed by his name and favorable articles in the press.

Work began in 1882, and it rapidly became clear that Lesseps had seriously underestimated the difficulties of building the canal. His general contractor, a Belgian firm, opted out after less than a year in the face of malaria and yellow fever epidemics that scythed through the ranks of workers, and the rocky Culebra that became unstable after every tropical rain and slid back into excavations as fast as they were made. By 1885, the Culebra had hardly been dented and costs were skyrocketing. Lesseps requested government authorization for a bond issue with a special lottery provision to spur public response. The government refused.

Desperate, Lesseps approached Eiffel in November 1887 and asked him to take over construction of the Panama Canal. Not only had Eiffel's perception of the task been right from the start, but also he had patented a system of metal locks that could handle differences of water level as great as 70 feet. Thus despite the animosity between the two men as a result of Eiffel's vote against Lesseps' sea-level plan, Eiffel plainly was the only hope left for the canal. Besides, Lesseps badly needed more capital. A new sale of bonds to the public might succeed if the great engineer's name were associated with the project.

Eiffel hesitated fully three weeks. Then he signed a $27.4 million contract with the Universal Interoceanic Panama Canal Company, as it had been renamed, to oversee all aspects of canal construction and to design, produce and install 10 locks. Considering that Lesseps had been floundering in the swamps of Panama for six years and the work was still barely begun, the deadline Eiffel accepted for completion and opening of the canal was, to say the least, astonishing: July 1, 1890 — only 30 months to push a canal through the treacherous isthmus, including a system of locks that had never been tried on such a scale. And the job was to be financed by a company that had been plagued with money problems since its founding. For once, Eiffel's prudent judgment appears to have been clouded.

But he was committed to the job and began executing it in January 1888 with his customary thoroughness and speed. The

The tower rises: January 1888 (Collection Tour Eiffel)

giant locks, sliding metal gates 79 feet wide, 69 feet high, and 13 feet thick, were subcontracted to a firm in Nantes, on France's Atlantic coast. Altogether they would enable a ship to be raised or lowered 330 feet, the maximum difference between Atlantic and Pacific.

By February he had 2,500 workers on the Panama site; by August over 6,000. As of August 25, 1888, barely eight months after taking over the job, Eiffel had excavated 630,000 cubic yards of earth and was in that respect nearly 10 months ahead of the schedule called for in his contract. He had on order 30,000 tons of cast iron for the locks, as well as 28,000 tons of cement and 26,000 tons of crushed stone for the masonry parts.[9]

Never had prospects appeared so favorable. In June the government had authorized Lesseps to float the bond issue refused three years earlier, bringing the company $51 million in new capital. For the first time since the project got under way eight years earlier, it began to look very much as if the Panama Canal, coveted for centuries by many nations, would after all be French.

April 1888 (Collection Tour Eiffel)

In Paris, the completion of the first platform in March 1888 gave Eiffel his launching pad for the rest of the tower. The first thing he did to prepare for the final phase of the ascent to 1,000 feet was to set up a steam-powered crane on the platform to hoist materials from the ground. Tracks were laid around the platform's circumference. Wagons like miniature boxcars carried materials from the central crane to the four creeper cranes.

June 1888 (Collection Tour Eiffel)

Workers were putting in 12-hour days during the spring and summer. To obviate their having to descend to the ground for lunch, losing more time each day as the tower rose, Eiffel installed a canteen on the platform. This had the additional advantages of preventing excess fatigue, and giving Eiffel a measure of control over on-the-job drinking, a common problem on French work sites.

The second level was reached in early July 1888, and on the 14th, Bastille Day, a fireworks display was shot off from the new height to the pleasure of crowds gathered across the Seine at the Trocadéro. That day, Eiffel held a banquet on the first platform for the Paris press. He took the occasion to deliver a pep talk.

"Judging by the interest that the tower seems to inspire both in France and abroad," he declared, champagne glass in hand, "I believe it is fair to say that we are showing the world that France continues to be the leader of progress, and that she is realizing a project which has often been tried or dreamed of. Only through the advancement of science, metallurgy and the art of engineering that distinguish the latter part of our century have we been able to surpass the generations that preceded us. Construction of this tower will be one of the landmarks of modern industry that made it possible."[10]

The sentiment was pure Victorian, the rhetoric probably a mix of conviction and press-agentry. Even so, Eiffel, an imaginative engineer but never one to strain for original phrasing when a platitude would do, once again showed a canny understanding of what the tower meant to his country, and what it would eventually mean to a newly technophilic world.

February 1889

Technical Challenge

IT WOULD BE FINE to have a thousand-foot tower as centerpiece of the 1889 World's Fair, but that in itself wasn't enough. The public had to be able to go to the top, and there was the rub. In fact, the tower's passenger elevators were one of the biggest headaches Eiffel had. In this area he had to rely entirely on subcontractors, and appears to have felt considerable frustration at seeing this major element escape his control. The Exposition committee was particularly concerned about the safety of the elevators.

While many visitors would likely be willing to climb the 363-step staircases in the east and west piers to the first platform, they could not be expected to go much farther on foot—it was another 381 steps to the second platform. A narrow spiral staircase of 927 steps led from the second level to the top, but was for use by the tower's personnel only. Fast, comfortable elevators were essential to the public's enjoyment of the tower, but the committee insisted first and foremost that Eiffel give every guarantee of their absolute safety. Casting worried glances over his shoulder on every decision about elevators, it reserved the right to veto any design that did not appear to meet its unconditional requirements.

Several factors compounded the problem of getting visitors to the top, with intermediate stops at the first and second levels. To begin with, the height to be scaled was far greater than any ever attempted. So too were the numbers of passengers to be transported—thousands per day if visitors were not to be discouraged by long waiting lines.

But the nub of the technical challenge lay in the tower's curving piers, where the elevators were to be installed. This required a design different from the usual straight vertical approach, or even a straight incline. From a ground-level angle of 54 degrees, the piers arched to 78 degrees at the second platform. The elevators would have to travel either on tracks with a constant curvature, or on tracks that approximated two straight runs at different angles. In neither case did the past experience of elevator makers in Europe or America provide a ready answer to the problem.[1]

The state of the art was primitive. Steam-power hoists, mainly for freight, had come into use in the 1860s, but the cumbersome drums they needed to take up supporting cables limited them to a rise of only about 150 feet. Systems with a screw and traveling nut were slow and suitable only for low-rise lifts. The most practical elevators of the day used a cylinder and piston power source, with the piston moved by water pressure. Attached to the elevator's cables, which passed over a sheave at the top of the shaft, the piston had its action multiplied by pulleys to give the desired rise. This so-called hydraulic, rope-geared technique had been developed by the 1880s, mainly in America by the Otis Elevator Company.

But in the view of European engineers, it had one major drawback: the cabin was suspended from above rather than pushed from below. Just as suspension bridges were generally avoided in Europe in favor of arched ones, suspension elevators were considered less safe than the direct plunger type. These used a piston that rose and fell as a cylinder was filled or emptied with water. Linear descendant of an ordinary hydraulic press, the plunger elevator was proof against accident, but its rise was directly related to piston length. This was an awkward arrangement at best, and an impossible one in the case of the tower's lower elevators, since a 220-foot cylinder well would have had to be bored right through the masonry foundations.

As soon as the tower's construction began, Eiffel appointed an engineer to study the elevator problem. The study skipped the whole knotty question of getting to the second level and concentrated on the long but straight run from there to the top. For that it proposed a suitably complicated system involving a nut and bolt arrangement that would, in effect, screw the cabin upwards on a helicoidal shaft. There would be two cabins on parallel shafts, traveling in opposite directions to counterbalance each other. The most novel touch was that each cabin would be powered independently by an electric motor, an idea that was ahead of its time since electric power was not used in elevators until the turn of the century. The committee was not convinced, however. Wary of the scheme's complexity, noise, and electric power, it rejected it in mid-1888.

Eiffel contracted with two French firms for the relatively easier elevator jobs, ground to first level and second level to the top, both allowing a straight run. For the more difficult task of negotiating the curve to the second platform, however, no French firm bid on the job. This left Eiffel in a pretty fix: the Exposition's charter explicitly prohibited use of foreign equipment in constructing the tower, and the only candidate for the remaining contract bore the unfortunate name of American Elevator Company, the European branch of Otis.

Otis duly submitted a bid through its Paris office, Otis Ascenseur Cie. The committee duly rejected it. But when an extended bidding time expired without a French proposal, the committee gave in and awarded a $22,500 contract to Otis. Thus the tower's elevators would comprise three entirely different systems installed by three different companies. The efficiency of this was questionable, but ultimately it proved workable.

This difficulty in finding a smooth, rational way to transport visitors graphically illustrates how unprecedented was the tower as an engineering project. Viewed from a distance, the tower appears simple, like a force of nature, a graceful iron geyser shooting from the earth. But a closer look reveals it to be full of busy sleight of hand. Those magnificent circular arches between its legs, for example, that most visitors assume support the tower, actually bear no weight at all. With their stylized floral motif, their role is purely decorative—and psychological. Eiffel knew that the public would intuitively feel safe on a structure supported by traditional-looking arches, but feel less at ease with one resting only on curving pylons.

The scrambled scenario of the tower's elevator systems epitomized the project's complexity. To get visitors up to the first level, elevators in the east and west piers; to the second, one elevator in the north pier that stops on the way at the first level, and in the south pier another that runs only between the first and second platforms; above the second level, a double elevator to the top, requiring a change of cars at an intermediate level. Compared to the spare, intelligent economy that marks most of Eiffel's work, the tower's internal transportation looks conceptually cumbersome.

Technical problems aside, the elevator design was in good measure dictated by aesthetics, for Eiffel refused to consider elevators that rose straight from the ground up through the tower's center. Such a system would have spoiled the structure's uncluttered purity of line, distracting the eye with shafts, cables, and cabins from the arches and their forceful visual impression of wide-straddled space. He was certainly right on that count. And it must be said in favor of the systems finally adopted that, despite their clanking, Rube-Goldberg complexity, they did do the job: the trip to the top of history's tallest tower took only seven minutes, and 455 persons per hour could make it. At the lower levels, 1,800 per hour could be hoisted to the first level, 882 to the second.[2]

Of the three systems, the Otis was simplest in design: a hydraulic, rope-geared unit that had become standard since about 1880. It used a piston 38 inches in diameter attached to cables running through a huge tackle with five fixed and six movable pulleys. As water from a reservoir on the second platform forced the piston through a 36-foot-long cylinder, the cable-suspended, double-deck cabin was pulled along a set of rails that curved once at the first level to accommodate the increasing angle of the tower's leg. The result was fast—400 feet per minute—and quiet. The cocky Americans at Otis had in fact worked on the design for three years, confident long before getting the contract that the committee would end up accepting their bid.

Although the cabin was fitted with spring-loaded brakes that would automatically grab the rails and stop the cabin's descent if any of the six cables broke, a heated dispute developed between Eiffel and Otis over safety. Probably pushed by the timorous committee, Eiffel insisted that Otis use the rack and pinion safety system installed on many of Europe's mountain cog railways. The American firm objected that cogs would be noisy and would

The Otis elevator system. (Collection Tour Eiffel)

unnecessarily restrict speed. When Eiffel and an Otis representative from New York failed to agree, Otis simply threatened to withdraw. Nothing further was said and no cogs were installed.

To dispel any public fear, Eiffel conducted a dramatic test before the Otis elevators went into service. On one of them he replaced the steel cables with hemp ropes, then raised the cabin about 15 feet and cut the ropes. The automatic brakes caught and the 19-ton cabin descended slowly to its base.

Before work was over, Eiffel again crossed swords with the American company—and again lost. The contract called for elevators in the north and south piers to be operational by January 1, 1889. Because of the number of modifications, Otis found this impossible, but guaranteed that they would be functioning by May 1, the fair's opening day. Eiffel threatened to refuse payment for work that did not meet the contractual deadline.

That prompted an enraged Charles Otis to set the trans-Atlantic telegraph cable sizzling with a message: "After all else we have borne and suffered and achieved in your behalf," Otis fumed, "we regard this as a trifle too much; and we do not hesitate to declare, in the strongest terms possible to the English language, that we will not put up with it." He threatened once more to quit—"and Mr. Eiffel must charge to himself the consequences of his own acts."

The ultimatum left Eiffel outgunned and with no alternative but to pay. He got his money's worth in the end. Although the Otis machines missed their May 1 deadline and were not both working until mid-June, they worked so well that they were considered one of the most effective American technical exhibits at the Exposition.[3]

French elevator makers were represented by two companies: Roux, Combaluzier and Lepape for the elevators in the east and west piers to the first level, and Edoux for the vertical run from the second platform to the top. Both systems were ingenious.

True to French prejudice against suspension elevators, Roux engineers opted for a technique resembling the direct plunger method. Since a 220-foot cylinder well was impracticable, they found a way to push up the cabin with what was in effect a flexible piston. Their solution was a chain of three-foot-long articulated links running through an iron conduit. Rollers in each link's joints were intended to reduce friction within the conduit, but succeeded only marginally. Powered by hydraulic cylinders similar to those used by Otis, large sprockets at the tower's base fit like gears into the links to force them up or to let them descend at a regulated pace under the weight of the cabin. It was extremely complicated, and the hundreds of links rolling through the conduit produced both excessive friction and noise.

But for Eiffel, who seems to have known a thing or two about public relations, the system was "not only safe, but appeared safe, a most desirable feature in elevators traveling such heights and carrying the general public." The unwieldy system was never used anywhere else.[4]

Eiffel still had to get the most ambitious visitors to the top. He awarded the contract to Léon Edoux, a schoolmate at Centrale and a leading French elevator manufacturer. Edoux's specialty was the plunger system, but the problem of installing a piston elevator with a rise of 526 feet was, like most of the tower's technical challenges, unprecedented. Not only was the length of rise over twice that of the highest piston elevator then in service, but aesthetics dictated that the plunger cylinder not infringe upon the open areas beneath the platforms. If a piston were placed at the bottom of the run, the second level, its cylinder would have to go all the way to the ground and then some—burying itself 146 feet deep in the middle of the base area. Such an eyesore was unthinkable.

Edoux's solution was a compromise between the piston and cable-suspended systems. He divided the vertical run into two equal parts and used two cabins, one ascending the first 263 feet and the other continuing to the top. Twin pistons pushed the cabin to the top, and since they were only 263 feet long they would not project below the second platform. With the two runs parallel but on either side of the tower's central guide rail, the cabins, connected by steel cables running over sheaves at the top, counterbalanced each other. Thus the cabin running from the intermediate level to the top rested on pistons, but the other one was suspended.

Given the French prejudice against suspension systems, this must have given the committee—and maybe Eiffel—some uneasy nights. But with four steel cables rated at over 2 million pounds of breaking stress and the maximum load possible being only 47,000 pounds, the safety factor was 43, enough to satisfy even the most punctilious engineer.

The tower's elevators turned out to be Eiffel's knottiest problem because the technology was so new. Engineering experts on the committee's technical council knew little about it. The same was true of Eiffel, beyond what he could understand in terms of basic mechanical engineering. He could guarantee on his own authority that his structure would stand. He could not say with the same certainty that none of the elevators would fail, for he had had no hand in designing them. But he was satisfied that the makers' calculations, at least, were right. The ultimate responsibility was his. The committee, we may imagine, kept its fingers crossed.

The Roux–Combaluzier elevator with its system of articulated rods. (Collection Tour Eiffel)

Seven

"Gloire à Monsieur Eiffel!"

As THE TOWER ROSE, so did pay for its builders. During the first 12 months of construction, pay rates ran from the equivalent at the time of eight cents an hour for unskilled laborers to 14 cents an hour for qualified metalworkers. In July 1888, wages for both categories rose by one cent, followed by another one-cent raise in September. In addition, Eiffel now assumed payment of accident insurance, which until the first platform was reached he had paid by withholding 2 percent of workers' pay.

But as the tower neared two-thirds of its ultimate height, worker unrest grew, reinforced by awareness that the Paris Exposition could not very well open with its vaunted tower half-finished. Admittedly, work had often been arduous and not without danger and discomfort. Vertigo seems not to have troubled the workers; wooden platforms had been built out around their positions to help them avoid seeing straight down.

Still, a fall was always possible. Besides the danger of death, there were the usual hazards of outdoor construction work, often magnified by the tower's height and its deliberately open design that afforded slight shelter from wind. During the winters of 1888 and 1889, workers perched on girders hundreds of feet above the Seine suffered from icy winds. Fingers froze to metal and rivets cooled before they could be driven.

When construction began, French labor was just beginning to become conscious of its potential power. Whereas there were on the average only 40 strikes per year in France between 1874 and 1880, the figure rose to 175 for each year from 1886 to 1889. Labor unions had been legalized in 1884. The tower was a vulnerable target for a strike; soon after the first platform was finished, worker representatives began demanding higher hourly rates.

On September 19, with working days growing shorter and pay packets shrinking as a result, tower workers downed their tools. The whole, finely coordinated operation came to a halt. They demanded a flat raise of four cents an hour for all categories of workers, applicable immediately. Eiffel countered with a proposal for a one-cent per hour raise for skilled workers only. After three days of bargaining, a progressive formula was worked out under which all workers would receive one cent per hour more each month, up to a maximum of four cents' increase.

Work resumed on this basis until mid-December, when the tower stood at 645 feet.

With raises under the September formula reaching their limit and Paris temperatures heading for their annual minimum, work stopped once again.

This time Eiffel refused to budge on salaries, although he promised a special bonus to all workers who stayed on the job until the tower was completed. Workers not present the following day would be fired. Most did show up, and the few who did not were easily replaced. Strike leaders—this was the 19th century—were taken off assembly jobs on the upper reaches of the tower, put to work building the first platform arcades, and forbidden to go higher. It was a calculated slap at their professional pride. Sarcastically called *les indispensables* by the other workers, most eventually quit their jobs. Thereafter the tower was free of labor strife. When it was finished, Eiffel had the names of 199 loyal workers, from Alézy to Zettelmaier, painted on a girder in full public view.

From the foundations to the second level, the tower is composed of four quadrangular piers joined into a rigid whole by horizontal bands of girders beneath each platform. From there to the top, however, the four distinct piers converge at a point slightly above the second platform into a single vertical column formed by their exterior faces. Thus there were no longer four creeper cranes to follow the tower's ascent, and Eiffel had to alter his method of

Work on the Exposition grounds as the tower reaches its second platform, July 1888.
(Collection Tour Eiffel)

rapidly getting the girders, rivets and other materials into position for assembly. His solution was to put new cranes on the vertical beams rising in the center of the tower that later would guide elevators to the third platform.

Placed back to back, the cranes counterbalanced each other and had enough reach to service all points of the tower's converging sides. To give them sufficient support on the narrow column, auxiliary iron frames 30 feet long and 12 feet wide were bolted to it and the cranes attached to them. When the two cranes had traveled up the 30-foot stretch, another frame was placed atop the first and the cranes clambered on. Time required to make the shift from one frame to another was only 30 hours, a quick operation considering that the cranes and their frames weighed 50 tons.

Eiffel now had four hoisting systems operating simultaneously: a steam winch on the first platform raising material from the ground, another on the second platform relaying it on to a third winch set on an intermediate platform at 650 feet, which passed materials and whole, prefabricated truss panels to the swiveling creeper cranes. A three-ton girder could be hoisted into position in only 20 minutes. This system was key to Eiffel's technique as he raced against the opening day deadline.

By now the tower was drawing an increasing number of curious visitors as eager for a view of Paris never before seen, except by a few balloonists, as for a look at the structure itself. One made the climb on a blustery winter day and duly recorded his impressions in the mauve prose still affected by French newspapers, incidentally giving us some insight into Gustave Eiffel's climbing prowess:

> Indian file, with Monsieur Eiffel in the lead, we start up the staircase. At that moment the thermometer says minus 1 degree centigrade. The weather is still threatening, but snow has stopped falling. Monsieur Eiffel advises me to imitate his gait. He climbs slowly, with his right hand on the banister. He swings his body from one hip to the other, using the momentum of the swing to negotiate each step. Here the incline is so gradual that we can chat as we climb, and no one is winded when we reach the first platform.
>
> At this height the city already appears immobile. The silhouettes of passersby and fiacres are like little black spots of ink

in the streets. Only the rippling Seine seems still alive. To the south there is a fine view of the fairgrounds, with the glass roof of the Machinery Hall looking like a lake of molten lead. I peek through a crack in the wooden flooring and look straight down into the void. Far below, I can see very small ducks swimming in a half-frozen pond. A shiver runs down my spine at the thought of a possible fall from this height.

Continuing up the stairs, the cold iron railing hurts my fingers so much that I try to climb with my hands in my pockets, but the wind buffets me and I am blinded by driving sleet. So I grab the railing again and shield my face with my arm. All I can see is Monsieur Eiffel's coat ahead.

At the height of 900 feet there is a wind of only 15 miles per hour, but it is enough to take my breath away. Workers here are placing a rivet. The great nail is taken red-hot from its portable forge, positioned in the hole and struck with heavy hammers in a shower of sparks. Below, Paris seems to be sinking into the night like some fabled city descending to the bottom of the sea amid a murmur of men and church bells.

We return to the second platform for hot drinks in the canteen. Monsieur Eiffel says that congratulations are coming in from all over, even from some of the artists who signed the famous protest. "There are only three or four stubborn writers still holding out," he says. "I really don't understand why."

Conversation drags on lazily. We are reluctant to leave the warmth of our shelter to go back into the wind, which seems to weep with the sound of human sobs in these hundreds of feet of iron stretched from earth to the clouds like an eolian harp.[1]

IT WAS TIME, in early 1889, to put the finishing touches on the tower. Most of the work went into the first level, where the majority of visitors were expected to stop. Open in the middle, the platform consisted of a rectangular promenade area 930 feet long and nine feet wide, sheltered by nine decorative arches on each side.

Here the public would get its first panoramic view of Paris and the fair, buy souvenirs and eat a meal at one of the tower's four restaurants, each with a different style and cuisine. Brébant, one of the best restaurants in Paris, opened a branch with a Louis XV décor; its terrace offered one of the best views of the fairgrounds. Opposite it, facing the Trocadéro Palace across the Seine, was an Alsace-Lorraine restaurant; a Russian-style bistrot faced the center of Paris, and on the fourth side was, oddly enough in culinary terms, an Anglo-American place.

On the second platform, workers were setting up a printing press and editorial room for *Le Figaro*, which would publish a special daily edition covering Exposition events. Here gastronomy was limited to a bar and a pastry shop. The center was taken up by the Edoux elevator.

Above, the octagonal third platform was being completely enclosed behind glass windows to protect visitors from wind. A short spiral staircase led up from there to a small apartment, including rooms reserved for scientific experiments, that Eiffel had built for his own use. On the balcony running around the platform, tracks were laid to carry two high-powered spotlights with a range of seven miles; they could be wheeled around to illuminate different monuments in the city for the pleasure of those on the tower.

At the tower's summit there was also a beacon with a range of nearly 120 miles, meaning the tower could be seen from as far away as Chartres and Orléans. The beacon's electric lamp was enclosed by a cylinder containing colored prisms giving off flashes of France's blue, white and red national colors as they revolved every 90 seconds. Protecting the tower from storms were eight lightning rods connected to iron conduits three inches thick running down the east and west piers to ground deep in the earth.

All along its height, the tower was getting a coat of reddish-brown paint imaginatively termed Barbados Bronze. Deep-toned on the lower piers, the color was progressively lightened until it was nearly pale yellow at the top, accentuating the visual impression of height. At the first level, Eiffel decided to paint the names of 72 French scientists who had distinguished themselves since the Revolution in 1789. This "invocation of science," as he called it, reflected his worry over accusations that the tower was useless and wasteful. The names of Ampère, Daguerre, Gay-Lussac and more than 60 others in gilded letters two feet high all around the tower would, he hoped, convince critics that the thing had a nobler purpose than to titillate the masses.

Eiffel was not only pained, as Le Corbusier said, by a lack of recognition of his aesthetic sense; he seems to have abhorred the idea that his thousand-foot tower might be considered fundamentally frivolous. He attempted to lay to rest any such notion during an address to a professional society in Paris in late February. "Besides its soul-inspiring aspects," he contended, "the tower will have varied applications for our defense, as well as in the domain of science." Heedless of protesting too much, he went on to list what he saw as the tower's potential uses:

> Strategic operations: in case of war or siege, it would be possible to watch the movements of an enemy within a radius of 45 miles, and to look far beyond the heights on which our new fortifications are built. If we had possessed the power during the siege of Paris in 1870, with its brilliant electric lights, who knows whether the outcome of that conflict would not have been entirely changed?
>
> Meteorological observations. It will be a wonderful observatory for studying the direction and force of atmospheric currents, the electrical state and chemical composition of the atmosphere, its hygrometry, etc.
>
> Astronomical observations: The purity of the air at such a height, the absence of mists which often cover the lower horizon in Paris, will allow many physical and astronomical observations which would normally be impossible in our region.
>
> Scientific experiments may be made, including the study of the fall of bodies through the air, resistance of the air according to speed, certain laws of elasticity, compression of gas and vapors, and, using a large-scale pendulum, the rotation of the earth. It will be an observatory and a laboratory such as has never before been placed at the disposal of scientists.[2]

As time went on, the tower *would* come to be taken seriously, occasionally by scientists but more often by painters, poets, and intellectuals who found in it an object of contemplation or a means of transcending the ordinary. Probably the first person to record the spell that the tower could cast on the unwary — particularly in an age when no one had ridden in an airplane — was a reporter from the usually solemn daily, *Le Temps*, who visited the monument in March 1889 as work was being finished. "Was it simply the weather that day, or do visitors always feel it?" he wondered:

> Whichever the case, an indescribable melancholy, a feeling of intellectual prostration took hold of me. At a height of 350 feet, the earth is still a human spectacle; an ordinary scale of comparisons is still adequate to make sense of it. But at 1,000 feet, I felt completely beyond the normal conditions of experience. At 350 feet one can admire the fact that such a puny being as man has accomplished the marvelous work that this infinite city represents; at 1,000 feet one no longer understands why man went to the trouble.[3]

At the end of March 1889, the tower topped out at 312.27 meters, including flagstaff, or 1,025 feet. Technicians were still tinkering with the worrisome elevators, but Eiffel's structural work was finished, two years, two months, and five days after it began. The tower was the world's tallest manmade object by far, making the runner-up Washington Monument look stubby by comparison. It would remain the tallest structure until completion of New York's Chrysler Building decades later.

Eiffel's execution had been marked by a deftness unique in the annals of great engineering projects until that time. His clockwork precision had enabled him not only to meet his deadline, but also to build the vertiginous structure with the loss of only one life, that of a worker who fell from the first platform while apparently showing off for his girlfriend after the bell had sounded ending the working day.

Such a safety record was phenomenal compared with other contemporary monumental works. The Brooklyn Bridge took some 20 lives including that of its designer, John Roebling. The death toll at the Forth Bridge was 57 workers, at the Quebec Bridge 84. And in a time when cost overruns plagued big projects nearly as much as they do today—the Brooklyn Bridge, for instance, cost twice the original estimate—Eiffel built his tower for exactly the equivalent of $1,505,675.90, or 6 percent *less* than the initial budget of $1.6 million.

On completion of his tower, Eiffel poses with his son-in-law, Adolphe Salles, on spiral staircase.
(Collection Viollet)

"Fruit of intuition, of science, of faith, daughter of courage and of perseverance," as Le Corbusier later called it, the tower was ready to be christened in that gusty early spring of 1889. Eiffel invited a few dignitaries such as Prime Minister Pierre Tirard, members of the Paris Municipal Council, and the Exposition's directors, Adolphe Alphand and Georges Berger, to a simple ceremony.[4]

Promptly at 1:30 P.M. on Sunday, March 31, he led the way up the north pier stairs with his hip-swinging climb. Most of the group dropped out, winded, at the first and second platforms. Eiffel and a few others, among them his veteran colleagues Emile Nouguier and Jean Compagnon, and the president of the Municipal Council, Emile Chautemps, reached the top a bit after 2 P.M. There Eiffel unfurled an appropriately grand French tricolor, 15 by 25 feet, emblazoned with the golden initials *RF* of the *République Française*, and ran it up the flagpole. Fireworks were set off on the second platform to resemble a 21-gun salute, rather as if the tower were a visiting sovereign.

Eiffel and his party descended, and he addressed the guests and about 200 workers. Toasts were proposed as champagne flowed, an excited Emile Chautemps crying, *"Gloire à Monsieur Eiffel et à ses collaborateurs! Vive la France! Vive Paris! Et vive la République!"*

In keeping with the unstated theme of the Exposition of 1889, Eiffel's speech was frankly patriotic, from the "great satisfaction" he felt at flying the French flag from the tallest edifice ever built, to the final moral: "You will remember always the great effort we have made in common to show all that, thanks to her engineers and her workers, France still holds an important place in the world, and that we are always able to succeed where others have failed, to the great honor of France and the Republic."[5]

Holding his top hat against the growing wind, Prime Minister Tirard made a brief reply, declaring that Eiffel was being promoted to the rank of officer in the Legion of Honor. The City of Paris also awarded a silver commemorative medal to all workers who had been on the site during the last months of construction.

Shortly after the ceremony, a violent spring storm swept across Paris from the northeast, lashing the city with rain, hail, and gale-force winds. Those who had tarried for a second glass of champagne scurried for shelter beneath the tower's arcades. Far above the Seine, the immense tricolor thrashed and whipped on its lacy, thousand-foot iron mast, but held.

Eight

Fair Star

MAY 6, 1889, was a brilliant spring day. The presidential carriage, a spanking new open landau, pulled away from the Elysée Palace shortly after lunch. It glided through the gilded gate known, from the strutting Gallic rooster on its top, as the Grille du Coq, and made its way up Avenue de Marigny beneath a profusion of white chestnut blossoms tall as paschal candles. A large crowd had turned out along the carriage's route across the Champs Elysées and into the fashionable Avenue Montaigne. Shouts of *"Vive Carnot! Vive la République!"* were answered with waves from the landau's three occupants, President Sadi Carnot, Prime Minister Pierre Tirard, and an aide-de-camp, Colonel Lichtenstein.[1]

With a detachment of cuirassiers leading the way, the little procession crossed the Iéna Bridge just as the 60th cannon shot of a 101-gun salute rang out. It entered the grounds of the Paris Universal Exposition, passed beneath the colossal arches of the Eiffel Tower, rolled on between colorful rows of honor guards from France's Asian and African colonies, and pulled up before the ornate iron and glass Central Dome, official entrance to the fair.

While most of France considered Carnot's appearance at the fair to be the inauguration of the centennial of the Revolution, the significant historical ceremony actually had taken place the day before. The States-General, which had transformed itself into France's National Assembly, thereby effectively ending the reign of Louis XVI, met at Versailles on May 5, 1789. On the eve of the Exposition's official inauguration, President Carnot had gone to the château a few miles southwest of Paris and placed a commemorative plaque in the room where representatives of the clergy, nobility and commons had gathered.

This ceremony was marred, however, for after reviewing troops from the Versailles garrison and watching the spectacle of the château's famous fountains, Carnot was the target of an assassination attempt. The shot fired by an apparently deranged man went wild. No harm was done except perhaps to the tottering image of the Third Republic, whose fall, one way or another, many considered imminent.

The Republic had survived 18 years, as long as any French government since the Revolution, narrowly escaping a coup d'etat the previous January by the dashing but irresolute monarchist, General Georges Boulanger, who at a crucial moment preferred to spend the evening with his mistress rather than take over the government. But despite pessimistic predictions by Left, Right and Center, the Third Republic was still on its feet for the opening of the long-awaited world's fair, as was President Carnot. (Carnot eventually did die by an assassin's hand, when he was stabbed to death three years later in Lyons by an Italian anarchist.)

The president entered the Central Dome at 2 P.M. to "The Marseillaise" as cabinet ministers and other VIPs filled stands beneath the dome. The diplomatic corps was also present, though with several notable absences. Except for neighboring Belgium, the royal courts of Old Europe adamantly refused to participate in what they considered France's exercise in revolutionary propaganda. Queen Victoria recalled her ambassador, Lord Lytton, to London lest his presence even anywhere near the fairgrounds be interpreted as endorsement. Similarly, no diplomats represented Austria-Hungary or Russia, and Germany sent only a lowly chargé d'affaires (though the German government later assigned several engineers to report fully on the Exposition, especially its iron structures).

The French government officially ignored the snub by the crowned heads, but the irreverent Paris daily *Le Petit Parisien* gave them the raspberry: "The kings are sulking, as usual," the paper editorialized. "What do we care! The people everywhere are on our side." And Britain's *Manchester Guardian* articulated what the British government dared not admit when it observed,

"The Exposition will be seen abroad as a visible sign of the extraordinary recovery of France."

When all were in their places beneath the 213-foot dome, Prime Minister Pierre Tirard, in his capacity as commissioner general, formally presented the fair to President Carnot. His speech was typical of the genre, reciting difficulties overcome and praising the foresightedness of the government. But if the Exposition itself was an elaborate rite in the industrial liturgy of 19th-century secular religion, one passage of Tirard's text could stand as its confident credo:

> Although this splendid result exceeds all our hopes, there is nothing in it that should surprise us. Progress never goes slowly; new generations constantly replace forces that are exhausted or have disappeared. Science—sovereign power of our century—does not stop the course of its research. Every day it penetrates further into the secrets of nature. Steam and electricity have already revolutionized the economic order of the universe—who can tell the prodigies and surprises they still hold for us and our descendants? Inventions, discoveries, improvements succeed each other with stunning rapidity. Nothing can resist this enormous push forward. Mills, workshops, factories, stimulated by competition, encouraged by success, undergo constant transformations of which we may be proud, for the result is an abundance of things necessary for life, the lessening of their prices, and consequently the increase of the general welfare.[2]

President Sadi Carnot, himself a graduate of Polytechnique and an engineer turned statesman, continued the theme of "a great century which has opened a new era in the history of humanity." After alluding to material and social progress since 1789, he stoutly defended France's right to hold the Exposition, foreign kings and critics notwithstanding: "Our dear France is worthy of attracting the elite of all peoples. She has the right to be proud of herself and to celebrate the economic and political centenary of 1789 with her head held high. . . . A century which has seen such miracles had to be celebrated."

The half-hour ceremony over, the president and his entourage began a two-mile walk through the fair's main attractions. The fair covered 228 acres, including exhibits on the Champ de Mars, the Esplanade des Invalides, along the Quai d'Orsay and in the Trocadéro gardens across the Seine from the Eiffel Tower. It was one-third larger than the previous fair in 1878.

The main show was on the Champ de Mars, starting with the tower and continuing through the magnificent Machinery Hall, the handsome domed buildings devoted to the fine and liberal arts, and industrial displays of all sorts. On the Esplanade des Invalides were military exhibits of the French War Department and the pavilions, in native architectural style, of France's colonies. An enormous building fronting the Seine along the Quai d'Orsay housed agricultural and food exhibits. The Trocadéro gardens were given over to horticulture.

While the fair's architecture consisted of the usual potpourri of styles found at such events, it was the first to make such bold use of iron, the Eiffel Tower being the most sensational example. In the important pavilions plaster, brick and stone had been banished in favor of iron girders, which were left visible to form the chief element of decoration. As in the Impressionist painting of the day, which deliberately attracted attention to how a work was put together, the composition of a structure was becoming the principal visual interest of architecture. In its self-assured use of iron, the Exposition of 1889 was more "modern" than the later Paris fair in 1900, which despite its permanent legacies to the city of the Grand Palais and Alexandre III Bridge, had already turned toward self-conscious academism.

The president's visit was a tumultuous affair, 800 policemen proving inadequate to control the opening day crowd of some 500,000 that streamed through the 22 entrances. Carnot was frequently jostled as he moved from one stand to another congratulating participants. Carnot took to his landau for the trip back to the Elysée Palace at 5:30 P.M., but Paris had only begun to celebrate.

The city was festooned with flags, bunting and miniature Eiffel Towers from the National Assembly to the Louvre, from the spires of Notre Dame to theaters, department stores, hotels and the facades of individual apartments. Tricolor banners flew from the scaffolding of the Sacré Coeur basilica, then being built as an expression of national contrition and hope and, like the tower, a reaction to the humiliation of the War of 1870. (Unlike the speed with which the tower was built, the ponderous masonry church would take all of 46 years to construct.)

When the small cannon on top of the tower sounded closing time at ten that evening, the festive public left the fairgrounds and lined the Seine to watch a Venetian-style show of brightly illuminated cruise boats slowly plying the river with orchestras playing on their upper decks. Above, the beacon on the tower flashed *bleu-blanc-rouge*, and two powerful spotlights at the top swung around at random to point long white fingers at various neighborhoods of Paris.

From time to time the tower's cannon boomed as colored flares were lit on all three platforms, bathing the bronze-colored latticework in sharp, surreal light. The evening climaxed with three gigantic fireworks displays fired simultaneously from the Tuileries, the Pont Neuf and the Ile des Cygnes. The pyrotechnics lasted an hour, regaling crowds with bombs set off high in the air from balloons, sparkling reproductions of Niagara Falls, and a flaming bouquet that morphed into a recognizable bust of President Carnot.

Meanwhile, the city's cultural elite was at the Comédie Française watching a verse play written in honor of the centenary. *The Song of the Century* was a heavy allegorical hymn declaimed by two actors representing Poetry and France. With fulsome exclamations it praised everything the Exposition stood for, and devoted particular attention to its star attraction:

> Clear-eyed Science and active Industry
> Have erected, among the spacious palaces,
> An iron Tower leading to the heavens.
> Unique, strange, and truly grandiose spectacle![3]

For another nine days the grandiose spectacle could be viewed but not visited. Eiffel's men were working overtime to put last-minute touches on the tower, but it took them until May 15 to have it in shape for the public, and even then the pesky elevators were not ready. In the first of its special editions composed and printed on the second platform, *Le Figaro de la Tour Eiffel* complained on May 15, showing that trench-coated journalistic self-dramatization is nothing new, "We have put together this number under rather special conditions: in a shack that barely covers our heads, amid carpenters, gas workers, blacksmiths and painters, dizzy from the unaccustomed air, dust and noise, and tired by the climb up the equivalent of 36 stories."

At 11:50 that morning, Eiffel, with evident relief, signed the guest book kept by the paper in its pocket-size editorial office. "Ten minutes to twelve, May 15, 1889. The tower is opened to the public. At last!"

The line of visitors that had begun forming an hour before starting moving up the stairs in the west pier to the first and second platforms. Despite the effort of the climb, during the following week nearly 30,000 persons paid the equivalent of 40 cents for a red ticket to the first level, and over 17,000 bought a 60-cent white ticket for the second. The first elevator to go into service was the clanking Roux Combaluzier model in the east pier on May 26, beating by a week the more sophisticated Otis model in the north pier. The second Otis was ready on June 16. At about the same time the $1 white tickets went on sale for the trip to the top in the Edoux elevator.

From then on the tower was, predictably, the fair's star. Huge crowds often waited hours in line for the opportunity to climb on it, ride on it, eat lunch or dinner on it, buy a souvenir, hold hands, and see from it a breathtaking panoramic view of the fair and the world's most beautiful city. In clear weather visibility reached to the Compiègne Forest 50 miles to the northeast, to Château-Thierry 40 miles to the east, to Fontainebleau 33 miles south and far into the rolling plains of Normandy to the west.

In theory, at least, the tower could accommodate 10,000 visitors at once: 400 in each of the four restaurants on the first platform,

The energy of Belle Epoque visitors to the tower was exceeded only by their elegance.

1,000 on the promenade areas of each of the four exterior galleries and 400 on the interior galleries between restaurants, 1,500 on the second platform and 500 at the top, plus 2,000 going and coming on the elevators and staircases. By the close of the Exposition, 1,968,287 persons had been up the tower, paying the equivalent of $1,142,834.70 in admissions. Some complained about having to pay the same price to climb up as to ride the elevators, but tower officials explained, with impervious Gallic logic, that this was "simpler." Visitors averaged 11,000 per day during the fair's 176 days, with a record 23,000 on the Whitmonday holiday, June 10.[4]

That was the day Eiffel opened the tower's guest book, or *Livre d'Or*, to cross-Channel nobility. Whatever Victoria might think of France's centenary, Arthur Edward, Prince of Wales and later King Edward VII, and his family visited the tower and took up one large page of the guest book with their flourishing autographs: besides the prince, there were Edward's wife, Alexandra, and their children, George, later George V, Victoria, and Maud, who became Queen of Norway.

Thereafter the tower frequently received VIPs. King George of Greece looked it over on July 22. At his request there was no ceremony, though personnel at *Le Figaro* chipped in and gave him a guidebook to Paris. On August 1 the Shah of Persia, Nasser Eddim, stopped at the foot of the tower during his tour of the Exposition. Not one to rush into the mysteries of modern technology, he waited on the ground while several of this lackeys made the ascent and returned to give their impressions. The Shah left, remarking only that the elevators made a good deal of noise. But he reconciled curiosity and caution two days later, when he returned to climb the stairs to the first level. He was rewarded with a special edition of *Le Figaro de la Tour Eiffel* printed in Persian, and he took the opportunity to buy two dozen miniature tower and a cane with a tower-shaped handle.

In late October Grand Duke Vladimir of Russia accepted a glass of champagne from Eiffel in the engineer's small apartment at the top, along with the likes of Prince Beloscowitz, Count Weil, and Duchess Josephine Melzi d'Eril of Milan. Among other notables on the tower that summer were the Khedive of Egypt, the King of

Siam, the Bey of Djibouti and of course the President of France, not to mention Buffalo Bill and Tom Tit, a midget clown. One message in the guest book, reading "Praise to Monsieur Eiffel with thanks from the Statue of Liberty, who owes him her iron skeleton," was signed Frédéric Auguste Bartholdi.

But one of the most enthusiastic visitors was Thomas Edison, whose phonograph, just then coming on the market, was among the most exciting and successful displays at the fair. The Wizard of Menlo Park ascended the tower several times. On August 13 he was accompanied by Eiffel's son-in-law, Adolphe Salles, and had himself photographed with Eiffel at the top. A month later Edison returned yet again to present one of his phonographs to Eiffel, thoughtfully including a recording of the chorus of the Paris Opera singing "The Marseillaise", which still stands in Eiffel's tower apartment. On this occasion Edison wrote in the guest book: "To Monsieur Eiffel the Engineer, the brave builder of so gigantic and original a specimen of modern Engineering, from one who has the greatest respect and admiration for all Engineers including the Great Engineer, the Bon Dieu."[1]

But the toffs had no monopoly on appreciation of the tower. Then as now, the masses responded to it with undisguised glee, appreciating it for what it basically is — a gigantic toy. They were excited when the miniature cannon on the top level was fired to mark the hour, the ladies cringing prettily and stopping their ears, top-hatted gentlemen assuming an air of martial stoicism. They took the restaurants by storm for the novelty of having lunch or dinner in the sky. They lined up on the second platform for souvenir copies of *Le Figaro de la Tour Eiffel* with the buyer's name quickly printed in the upper right corner with the date. By the thousands they signed their autographs and listed their hometowns in the guest book. Many added their impressions, but for clever (and untranslatable) word play few matched the amorous wit who wrote:

Eiffel, que j'adore la taille
De ta Tour,
Mais, Mimi, combien plus le tour
De ta taille!

This being the fashion capital of the world, smart young things had to have a special dress for the ascent. A fanciful number was duly whipped up for the occasion by a Paris shop. Known as the *Eiffel ascensionniste*, the outfit featured several superposed collars on the pretext of protecting the adventurous wearer against cooler temperatures at high altitude. Playful young women invented one of that summer's more popular pastimes when they tied messages to gas-filled balloons and released them from the top of the tower. Some of the notes were whimsical billets doux, but others requested that the finder reply. Answers came back from as far away as Belgium, Bavaria and Hungary.

Although the tower was only at the beginning of its career as the symbol of Paris, it was already everyone's favorite touchstone at the Exposition of 1889. It was not enough to visit the structure and play on it. The tower had to be taken home in one of the numerous forms on sale at souvenir stands all over Paris. Millions of miniature towers, tiny enough to be worn on charm bracelets or large enough to be made into reading lamps, left Paris for thatched cottages in Normandy and the four corners of the earth. An entire meal could be eaten under the sign of the tower, with tower-shaped bottle openers, dishes, silverware and salt and pepper shakers decorated with its image, wine and liqueur bottles molded in its form.

But the tower also inspired more, in those days of craftsmanship, than the gimcrackery found on sale in Paris today. Some of the plates decorated with its image were beautiful specimens of Limoges porcelain. Fine crystal wine glasses, their bases in the shape of the tower, were engraved with its outline in delicate filigree — today they can occasionally be had in Paris antique shops for upwards of $250. Huge conch shells were skillfully worked by artisans to produce exquisite cameos of the tower. Full-color pictures of it were enameled on ladies' expensive cosmetic cases and music boxes. Artists and philosophers would later point out the grip that the Eiffel Tower can exercise on the imagination; the public recognized that intuitively in 1889, willingly accepting the tower's reign over the fair. As one speaker at an international banquet during the fair put it, "Here we are all citizens of the Eiffel Tower."[6]

Visitors on the first platform deciding whether to go higher. (Collection Viollet)

The French are justly known for their national self-centeredness, which they themselves refer to as *nombrilisme* (literally, "navelism" as in closely studying one's own). But that year they could be forgiven a certain narcissism, for Paris did indeed seem the center of the universe. News of the great fair had reached practically every point on the globe, and visitors poured into the city, sometimes by the most diverse means of transportation. Most arrived by train, and the Saint Lazare station had been completely rebuilt for the occasion at a cost of $6 million. Its arrival hall now was 200 yards long and could accommodate thousands of travelers at a time when the boat trains from Le Havre arrived.

But a number of visitors eschewed conventional conveyances to Paris. One anonymous American crossed the Atlantic in a small sailboat. On a bet, two Austrians left Vienna in a wheelbarrow, taking turns pushing; they covered 750 miles in 30 days and won their bet. Another Viennese, a journalist, made the trip in 21 days in a rented hackney. One of the most talked about arrivals was that of Lieutenant Michel Assiev, a 25-year-old officer in the Russian dragoons stationed in the Ukranian town of Poltava. The intrepid lieutenant made the 1,600-mile trip to Paris on two horses in 30 days, averaging 11 hours per day in the saddle and losing 10 pounds in the process. Paris newspapers gave him a hero's welcome.

By any measure the Exposition was the most successful fair the world had ever seen. It attracted a paid attendance of 32,250,297, including an estimated 90,000 Americans, over twice that of the 1878 Paris world's fair, the biggest until then. The permanent population of Paris was swollen by an average of 200,000 every day during those six months; the city's businessmen happily estimated that visitors spent $324 million. Paris was transformed into a swirling vortex with the Eiffel Tower at its center. One of the few not caught up in the gaiety and hubbub was Guy de Maupassant, who continued to sulk:

> Beginning in early morning the streets are already full, the sidewalks flowing with crowds like swollen streams. Everyone is heading for the Exposition or is coming back or returning again to

it. In the streets, the carriages form an unbroken line like cars of a train without end. Not a single taxi is free, no driver will consent to drive you anywhere but to the fair. Besides, the only customers they want are the flashy foreigners. Impossible to find a table in a restaurant, and friends no longer dine at home or accept a dinner invitation to your home. When invited, they accept only on condition that it be for a banquet on the Eiffel Tower—they think it more amusing that way. As if obeying a general order, they invite you there every day of the week for either lunch or dinner.[7]

But even Maupassant would eventually come to admire the fair's show of France's newfound strength.

World on Display

On the Champ de Mars fairgrounds, something over 60,000 exhibitors had spent nearly $36 million to present their displays. Several of the 49 countries represented had constructed lavish buildings for their exhibits. The Central and South Americans in particular had made a special effort: Mexico's $1.2 million building was the most expensive, followed by the $1 million Argentinian pavilion. Bolivia, Nicaragua, Chile, as well as little San Salvador and Santo Domingo all had their buildings.[1]

Paradoxically, many nations with the most advanced industrial economies of the age did not erect their own pavilions. Germany remained sullenly behind the Rhine, the government discouraging firms from exhibiting and warning private citizens of a hostile reception by French citizens if they ventured to Paris for a look at the fair. Mammoths such as Krupp, the Continent's biggest maker of iron and steel products and railroad materiel, and Siemens, a leader in electrical and telegraphic equipment, were thus absent from the Exposition of 1889, although they had been outstanding exhibitors in previous Paris fairs. Great Britain was present unofficially in the form of exhibits by individual firms. But the total outlay for British stands was only around $100,000, about the same as the less-developed Belgium, Portugal, Romania or Japan.

The United States was present officially but did not erect a pavilion. The government allocated $250,000 to defray exhibitors' expenses and named General William B. Franklin, a prominent Union officer during the Civil War and later vice president and general manager of the Colt Patent Fire Arms Company, commissioner general of the exhibit. Due to a certain amount of bungling by Congress and the government, the American show at Paris was not what it might have been, as General Franklin pointed out in his final report.

In the first place, Congress dallied for over a year before accepting, in May 1888, France's invitation to participate in the fair. Then, the law that was passed accepting the invitation failed to authorize government departments—except the Department of Agriculture—bureaus and museums to send exhibits to Paris. Other complicating factors were a large centennial exposition in Cincinnati during the summer of 1888, making many firms reluctant to mount another costly exhibit the following year, and apprehension in the United States over possible political instability in France.

These complications, plus the fact that the United States was the last large industrial nation to apply for space, resulted in an American exhibit that was rather shabby compared with those of its better organized European competitors. Altogether the American displays covered some 86,000 square feet, mainly in the Machinery Hall, its arrangement left much to be desired, as the final report noted bitterly. Promised exhibits failed to arrive, leaving holes in the American section that had to be filled at the last second. Franklin's report stated:

> The resulting fortuitous assemblage of incongruous objects, located in an extensive gallery devoid of interior architectural features and of ornamental installations arranged according to a matured plan, produced anything but an imposing general effect. It can easily be understood how those who judge by the impressions received from the first view of an exhibition, without looking beneath the surface for the merits of the products, may have formed an erroneous estimate of the importance of the United States exhibit.[2]

Americans touring the exhibit were particularly disappointed by the railroad section, a stand that many said looked more like a railroad accident than a display of new equipment. On the whole, General Franklin concluded, "In comparison with the symmetrical arrangement and elegant installations of the French departments, our sections suffered greatly."[3]

Still, when Exposition officials handed out awards at the close, American exhibitors did exceptionally well, winning 55 grand prizes, 214 gold medals, and 300 silver medals. Grand prizes, for example, went to such diverse enterprises as American Bell Telephone, Thomas Edison, Stetson, Tiffany, McCormick Harvesting Machine Co., and that archetypal American business, the Winchester Repeating Arms Co. American supremacy in mechanical engineering was acknowledged by many international observers, including a Belgian jury member judging mechanical exhibits. Given Europe's top-down approach to most issues, its mental and social rigidity, and its seemingly ineradicable elitist education system with its corresponding loss of human potential, his observations are unfortunately just as valid today as then:

> One of the most striking facts that the Exposition of 1889 brings into relief is that, with respect to machinery, American influence is extending more and more and gaining a stronger foothold day by day in Europe. The United States has imposed upon us its forms, its methods of execution, even the organization of work by which more perfect precision is obtained in the production of its workshops, and in the case of steam engines it has imposed its types . . . Does not the difference we find lie in education? In the United States it is free everywhere, everywhere creative and expansive as freedom itself. In Europe it is regulated, powerfully organized, the work of a despotism smacking of the barracks.[4]

Two American exhibits attracted the most excited crowds during the entire six months of the Exposition. One was Thomas Edison's displays of phonographs and electric lighting. Phonographs with recordings and headsets were available for demonstration to the public, and lines formed early each day at Edison's stands in the Machinery Hall. Although one French critic found sourly that "the timbre of voice reproduced is more appropriate to a Punch and Judy show, and the static makes all charm and illusion impossible," most who tried on the headsets were enthusiastic.[5] "The phonograph faithfully reproduces the human voice," wrote another visitor to the stand, "clearly pronouncing even the most difficult diphthongs." The press announced solemnly that the august French

Academy planned to create a library containing the voices of all its "immortal" members: "One of the most prodigious advances of the future will be the ability to make the dead speak."[6]

The other popular American display, though not actually an exhibit, complemented Edison's by presenting the nonindustrial face of America. Billing itself on posters all over Paris as "*L'Attraction la Plus Grande du Monde*," Buffalo Bill's Wild West Company arrived at Le Havre on May 11. Just who William Frederick Cody was needed some explanation for Parisians. One newspaper undertook to clear up the matter with a highly imaginative thumbnail portrait: "Buffalo Bill, who will be our guest during the Exposition, is in a sense the Robinson Crusoe of the New World. Adventurous to excess and brave to the point of recklessness, he succeeds in his audacity and his whims through really extraordinary strength and suppleness. He is the descendent of a most aristocratic family."[7]

Costarring Annie Oakley, billed as "Queen of the Rifle," the company of cowboys and Indians set up on the western outskirts of the city and gave its first show on May 18 for a bemused President Carnot. Thereafter the show was packed afternoon and evening for the duration of the fair. On their off hours, the members appear to have done their share of sightseeing: the third person—and first American—to sign the guest book on the Eiffel Tower on May 15 was a gentleman named A. S. Hayne, who listed his home town as Fort Worth, Texas.

ALTHOUGH THE EIFFEL TOWER was the most popular structure at the fair, it was not actually the biggest. That title went to the Machinery Hall. A palace of iron and glass erected to the glory of steam power, of screws and gears and pistons and flywheels, the vast hangar had a nave 377 feet wide, the broadest space ever covered by a single span of roof until that time. With a length of 1,380 feet and lateral wings extending off the main hall, it enclosed nearly fifteen acres. Twenty enormous curved girders arched 160 feet above the exhibition floor to support a glass roof.

Impressed observers groping for comparisons found that Paris' Vendôme column could stand in the Hall and leave 23 feet above Napoleon's head; if the building were turned into an annex of the nearby École Militaire, there would be room to exercise 1,200 cavalry horses at a time. Total weight of the iron in it was 500 tons more than in the Eiffel Tower.

At the Paris Exposition of 1889 as at the industrial fairs that had preceded it, the Machinery Hall was the heart of the matter, a cornucopia filled with the most ingenious products of the industrializing world. Exhibits ranged from machine tools to mining machinery, from spinning and weaving machines to electrical and railway equipment. Most of the machines were in motion, powered by 32 steam engines providing over 5,000 horsepower through miles of underground conduits. Visitors who desired an overall view of this roiling sea of elbowing tie-rods and spinning whirligigs could ride on an electrically powered bridge spanning the central nave. Two hundred spectators could stand on it as it moved slowly from one end of the Hall to the other.

Among the Hall's exhibits was the world's first gasoline-powered automobile, a Benz. The car was still largely a curiosity for most visitors, whereas the variety of unicycles, bicycles and tricycles on view captivated a public then in love with what Parisians called *la petite reine*. A French company displayed its ambitious new steam tricycle, capable of attaining considerable speed, and of climbing steep grades despite its weight of 400 pounds. Exhibits of typewriters attracted almost as many eager spectators as Edison's phonograph; the relative merits of keyboard machines such as the Remington and single-key models like the Mercury created lively debate around the stands.

But while there was far more diversity in design of similar products than exists today, the series of international expositions held from 1850 to1900 began the move toward standardization, if not globalization. "Each nation," one observer noted, "gradually losing its prejudices, has adopted the improvements which have enabled another to take the lead in any particular direction, whether in matters of practical importance or of good taste. A general uniformity of excellence, amounting indeed to a certain lack of individuality in the design of the machinery of any one class, was a marked feature of the Exposition of 1889."[8]

The grand Machinery Hall itself succeeded almost too well in its awe-inspiring dimensions. It had ample room for the fair's plethora of exhibits, but critics remarked that its immensity dwarfed its contents. Compared with the building, even the largest machines appeared insignificant. Moreover, if the glass roof admitted needed daylight, its panes had a regrettable tendency to break during expansion and contraction of the iron framework due to temperature changes; this occasionally showered the floor with sharp shards.

Also, the Hall's designers had assumed that the great volume of enclosed space would make forced ventilation unnecessary. But with midsummer sunlight streaming in, heat on the exhibition floor often became unbearable in the afternoon. Thus most of those attending the fair were glad, once they had done their duty by compound locomotives and Westinghouse air brakes, to turn to more frivolous matters.

Next to viewing the fairgrounds from the Eiffel Tower, the best way to get a quick survey was to board one of the miniature trains that chugged for two miles around the perimeter of the Exposition. Composed of seven cars, including a closed *salon de luxe*, the trains left every 10 minutes from the Esplanade des Invalides and followed the Seine around to the Eiffel Tower, turning left there to the Machinery Hall. The highly popular little trains carried over 6 million paying passengers during the fair.

A more exclusive means of transportation through the grounds was rental chairs with comfortable wicker seats and spring suspension mounted on large rubber-tired wheels, pushed by uniformed attendants. These were particularly appreciated by *les élégantes* of Paris who disdained to scuff their dainty slippers on gravel paths, and wished to appear fresh for lunch on the Eiffel Tower.

This being Paris, eating was one of the more important activities at the fair. A tour of the huge food and agriculture hall, running for nearly a half-mile along the Quai d'Orsay, was a must. Food products from all over the world — including even English bread, which the French appear to have found intriguing if a bit

heavy—were on display, along with the latest model machines
for slicing, grinding and mixing food. In terms of size, the most
impressive single exhibit was a gargantuan oaken wine barrel
sent over from Epernay by one of France's biggest champagne
makers. Its head carved and gilded with rococo extravagance, the
barrel contained the equivalent of 20,000 bottles. Ten pairs of
oxen had drawn it to Paris on a route carefully planned to avoid
narrow bridges.

But food was not merely to be contemplated. When 18,000
mayors from the French provinces gathered in one wing of the
Machinery Hall for a banquet hosted by the government, they put
away a meal that would have daunted Rabelais: soup, trout, cold
beef filets, truffled hen, young roast turkey, spring salad, frozen
soufflés, chocolate cake and rum baba, accompanied by Madeira,
two Bordeaux vintages, one Burgundy, coffee and liqueurs.

The 50-odd restaurants, cafes, snack bars and buffets on the
fairgrounds were crowded daily to overflowing, and forewarned
families brought along well-filled hampers. Picnics of cold meat,
cheese, fruit and wine on the lawns and steps of exhibit halls soon
became one of the fair's popular impromptu activities. More exotic
gastronomic attractions were available in the Exposition's Rue du
Caire, a facsimile of a Cairo street, complete with bustling bazaars,
beggars demanding baksheesh, and donkey drivers beating their
animals. The street's cafes offered strong, bitter coffee and gummy
cubes of Turkish delight along with undulating belly dancers.

This was one of the most exotic world's fairs ever held. France's
colonial empire extended from Southeast Asia to West and North
Africa. The colonies' pavilions lining the east side of the Esplanade
des Invalides formed a colorful, jumbled world apart. Strollers
had their senses agreeably assaulted by the smell of Oriental
spices and North African couscous, the sounds of Senegalese
tom-toms, Polynesian flutes and Annamite gongs, the sight of
Moslem minarets and Cambodian temples.

In the bazaars of the large Algerian and Tunisian pavilions,
craftsmen fashioned jewelry, finely tooled leather and brightly
colored tapestries. Nearby, nubile young women from Java and
Tahiti performed native dances with an authenticity that some

prim observers found scandalous. Indeed, presence at the fair of thousands of natives from the colonies worried self-appointed monitors of public morality. A correspondent from one very proper Paris newspaper wrote, "I must demand supervision of these natives whose loose morals border on licentiousness. It appears that their behavior is due to an excess of innocence on their part. But they would be just as interesting if they were a little less innocent."[9]

But while the fair's emphasis was on industry, art also had its place. Beneath the handsome glazed tile dome of the Arts Hall, however, wall space was generally limited to the works of painters who adhered slavishly to the clichés of academic style. The jury that decided which works would be admitted was headed by Ernest Meissonier and Adolphe Bouguereau, two prominent members of the academic school that favored photographic realism and syrupy subjects.

Most Parisians, unaware of or frankly hostile to the wind of creative change called Impressionism, still doted on flowery hymns to spring, Virgins surrounded by rosy cherubs, a fleshy Bacchus in his cups. Another year would pass before a young French painter and critic named Maurice Denis boldly wrote in a Paris art magazine that "A painting, before being a warhorse, a naked woman, some anecdote or whatnot, is essentially a flat surface covered with colors arranged in a certain order." And despite the fact that no fewer than eight exhibits by Impressionists had been held in Paris in the previous 15 years, their work was represented by only a handful of canvases among the hundreds of paintings hung in the Exposition's official art pavilion.[10]

This omission led to one of the fair's livelier sideshows. Paul Gauguin, one of the most flamboyant artists of the day and leader of a small clan of painters who made their headquarters at Pont Aven in Brittany, went to a large cafe next to the Arts Hall and offered to decorate it with nearly 100 paintings and drawings by the Pont Aven group. The wall mirrors the owner had ordered had not arrived in time for the fair, so he agreed to hang the improvised art show.

Gauguin grandly named the exhibit the Impressionist Synthetist Group, strung a blue and white banner across the cafe entrance, and pasted posters all over Paris advertising the show. The enterprising cafe owner hired an all-women's violin ensemble to serenade the crowds as they streamed in to be titillated by the revolutionary inversed perspectives on the walls. Success of his rump exhibit assured though the press largely ignored it, Gauguin spent most of his time indulging his taste for South Pacific dancers in the fair's Javanese village. In 1891, he left for Tahiti.

Meanwhile, revolutionaries of another sort were meeting in Paris. Of the 70-odd international conferences held in conjunction with the Exposition covering subjects from criminal anthropology to medical jurisprudence, lifesaving to ballooning and carrier pigeons, the most significant in its long-term repercussions was the founding congress of the Socialist Party's Second International. Several of the objectives agreed upon by the congress — radical notions at the time — have become part of normal industrialized economic and political life: eight-hour workdays, universal manhood suffrage and selection of May Day as the occasion for a demonstration of working-class strength. Interestingly for disciples of Marx, May Day was proposed not by European ideologues, but by the pragmatic American Federation of Labor; the motion passed despite objections by the German delegation that it was too provocative.

Electricity, just beginning to replace the melancholy yellow gaslights along Paris streets, made the Exposition of 1889 the first world's fair to remain open in the evening. The Eiffel Tower was illuminated by thousands of electric bulbs; the pavilions and gardens on the fairgrounds were garlanded with strings of lights. And at nine every evening began one of the fairgoers' favorite shows, a brilliant display of luminous fountains.

Folding chairs surrounding the monumental allegorical fountain representing "France Steering the Ship of Progress" were occupied hours before the first jet of vibrantly colored water shot 60 feet into the air. Located squarely in the middle of the Champ de Mars between the Eiffel Tower and the Central Dome, the fountain by day was a triumph of pompous academic sculpture. France, a plump, winged lady raising a torch in her right hand, steered the ship of the Republic, with a crowing Gallic cock on its prow, as lissome young things named Science, Art and Progress cheered her on. At night, all this could be overlooked as columns, curtains and corollas of water spurted from nozzles in a reflecting pool 120 feet long and 50 feet wide.

Illuminated from the pool's bed by a complex system of electric lights behind colored lenses, the fountains seemed to hurl glowing rubies, diamonds, pearls, sapphires and emeralds at the evening sky. The show lasted 20 minutes, nozzles and lights shifting and combining to produce changing patterns of ever more grand effect. Few of those who applauded this further evidence of French genius were aware that it was the creation of the British firm of Galloway and Sons, who previously had built similar fountains in London, Manchester and Glasgow.

THE PARIS EXPOSITION of 1889, scheduled to close officially on October 31, stayed open an extra week to satisfy popular demand before it was finally turned over to the demolition crews. The French government, thoroughly pleased with its centennial, held a formal closing ceremony on Sunday, September 29, at which it awarded grand prizes, medals and diplomas to some 33,000 exhibitors. The centennial's economic and political themes had been well served by the fair, President Sadi Carnot said in his closing remarks, adding, "Here has been shown the glorification of the work of 1789, the emancipation of industry, and a complete picture of one of humanity's greatest economic and social revolutions."[11]

Prime Minister Pierre Tirard took the occasion for a final potshot at the Exposition's critics: "This coincidence of the celebration of the centennial of the Revolution of 1789 with a great international exposition is not, then, as seems to have been believed by some, a sterile political manifestation, but is really the demonstration of the power and vitality of a free nation."[12]

The Third Republic, which only a few months before had seemed on the verge of a coup, was stronger than ever. Many were convinced that this new "power and vitality" was due in good part to the overwhelming success of the fair. It had convinced the French themselves that a democratic government was viable after all. Even the sullen Maupassant grudgingly acknowledged that the fair "has shown the world, just when it needed to be shown, the strength, the vigor, and the inexhaustible wealth of that surprising country: France."

On the international scene, too, France had made her point. Henceforth she would be taken seriously in the industrial world. A German journalist, returning home after visiting the fair, wrote:

> We have been only too inclined to see French industrial spirit in decline. That is a fatal error, as this Exposition proves strikingly. The giant structures on the Champ de Mars and the Esplanade des Invalides, with their huge and richly filled galleries, are proof that the French capacity for work has not been idle for a single moment, and that this nation is firmly resolved to reconquer its preponderant place in world markets.[13]

Commissioner William B. Franklin of the American exhibit was similarly impressed. In his final report he declared his admiration for what France had managed to bring off:

> Everything connected with the Exposition convinces an intelligent observer that the nation which could thoroughly organize so grand a work must at least be abreast of all modern nations in works of industry and art, and in the ability to organize and utilize the brains and muscles of its people.
>
> Whatever may have been the reputation of France before the Exposition in these respects, it must be acknowledged that no other nation in the world could at this time have equaled France in its display of modern fine arts or could have exceeded it in any other department of the Exposition; and it is certain that no such great result, due to ability of administration and energy of purpose and to the enormous wealth of objects—the results of industry and art—has ever been attained by any other nation or can be surpassed in the near future.[14]

But the fair's most lasting legacy was neither economic nor political; rather, it was an utterly superfluous thousand-foot iron tower. Fortunately the tower stood in Paris, a city whose inhabitants have always recognized the human need of the superfluous. This insured that the tower would have a long and profitable life, certainly longer than anyone—except perhaps Gustave Eiffel—expected in 1889. As for profitability, revenues during the fair in addition to the initial government subsidy were sufficient to cover the tower's cost. Eiffel was able to pay off the bondholders that first year of the tower's existence; it has been a money-maker virtually ever since.

Well on its way to becoming the world's best-known landmark, the tower had already made converts of most of the vociferous band of writers and artists who had opposed it. The composer Charles Gounod, for example, attended a little party one summer evening in Eiffel's tower-top apartment, singing and playing the piano until 4 A.M. For such special guests Eiffel kept an autograph book in the form of a folding fan decorated with views of the tower. He himself had proudly written on it, "The French flag is the only one to have a staff a thousand feet tall." Gounod in turn wrote, "The man who could put an army of workers a thousand feet in the air deserves at least a pyramid," and jotted down a tune to go with the message.

Intended as a souvenir for Eiffel's daughters, the fan also recorded the change of heart of another protester, Ernest Meissonier, who praised Eiffel's feeling for the changing light of the Paris sky—"an engineer who speaks like an artist." Succeeding folds were covered by such as Frédéric Mistral, the poet of Provence, who scribbled a little ditty, and Thomas Edison. Ten days later, Edison would salute Eiffel in the guest book as a "brave builder." But on August 30, the American inventor summed up his enthusiasm for the tower in a phrase of peculiar resonance: "The Eiffel Tower is one of the gravest things done in modern engineering."[15]

Belle Epoque or Fin de Siècle?

BOTH TERMS, Belle Epoque and fin de siècle — the former connoting the pleasurable good life, the latter a world-weary, decadent society — are used to describe the life of Paris following the great Exposition of 1889. Both, to varying degrees, are accurate.

Certainly the 1890s were a time of effervescent creativity in the arts, of uninhibited enjoyment of the infinitely variegated pleasures of the capital, of easy assurance that man was master of his fate. Equally surely it was an age of social and cultural leveling, of sordid poverty among the growing industrial proletariat, and of bomb-throwing terrorism by anarchists. The French revolutionary Saint-Just had said that happiness was "a new idea in Europe". That often treacherous idea had catalyzed the agitated first century of industrialization, and seemed to reach a frenetic climax in the last decades before Europeans again began slaughtering each other in the First World War.[1]

"I hope you may come to know a time like my youth," wrote Paul Poiret, the style-setting Parisian couturier who was born in 1879, "when people could enjoy the present because they had confidence in the future. The petty worries and annoyances of life had not yet crushed the individual and put a damper on the pleasures of life."[2]

Pleasure, intellectual as well as physical, was the operative word of Belle Epoque Paris, then a city of 2,500,000. "I would be very stupid not to extract from life what it gives us on the instant," wrote the playwright Jules Renard, adding that when he met a friend on the boulevard, he would toss him a new idea rather than simply make small talk, "thus making of what would have been an exchange of banalities, a discussion that enriches the day."[3]

Merely to stroll down the *Grands Boulevards* from the Madeleine church on past the Opéra was to sample the city's joie de vivre. A glimpse of the latest fashions and an exchange of lively gossip went with a *fine à l'eau* (brandy with a dollop of water) at any of the cafes — as many as 2,500 tables lined the sidewalks on summer days — where the worlds of politics, theater and journalism met.

The cafe had been an important Paris social institution since the Second Empire, when Tortoni, on Boulevard des Italiens, attracted a fashionable set headed by literary luminaries such as the poet Alfred de Musset, the novelist Alexandre Dumas, and the aristocratic gadfly Duc de Morny. By the nineties, tastes had changed and Tortoni closed in favor of the nearby Napolitain and a dozen others, including some still extant like the Café de la Paix.

With a few exceptions, such as the Jockey Club, private men's clubs had never flourished in Paris as in London — French men enjoy the company of their womenfolk — but many Parisian males felt the same sort of allegiance to their cafes. It was said that a man would change his religion sooner than his cafe, and the poet Jean Moréas thus described the boulevardier's day: "You arrived at your cafe at 1 P.M. and stayed until seven. You went out for dinner. You came back at nine and stayed until 2 A.M."[4]

Cards and dominoes were played in the cafes, letters and poems were written on the marble-topped tables, and a usually moderate amount of drinking went on. But the main pastimes were conversation — the wittier and more malicious the better — and the political intrigue that doomed the life expectancy of a Third Republic government at this time to about 12 months.

On the other side of Paris, the Bois de Boulogne attracted the glittering carriages of the worldly *monde*, as well as the less respectable but much appreciated *demi-monde*, from the likes of Baroness Adolphe de Rothschild escorted by grooms in cockaded hats, to a bejeweled courtesan or "Grand Horizontal," as they were delicately known, such as Emilienne d'Alençon or La Belle Otero out of their perfumed boudoirs for a breath of air.

Gentlemen settled questions of honor with pistols or swords in the Bois — dueling was not outlawed until after the First

A Belle Epoque caricature of Eiffel published in the English humor magazine Punch.

World War—often retiring to their favorite cafe for a drink if, as frequently happened, both participants escaped unscathed. Automobiles were beginning to frequent the wood's earthen paths, on some days to the point where, as one contemporary noted with distaste, "the harsh smell of gasoline obliterates the noble smell of horse manure."[5]

Dandies and dilettantes expressed their contempt for the benighted but burgeoning middle class with such extravagances as Boni de Castellane's Palais Rose, a lavish town house in pink marble near the Arch of Triumph reputed to be the most sumptuous private residence of the late 19th century. Like many Paris aristocrats, Boni scorned electricity as a gadget for the nouveaux riches and lit his palace—from the ballroom to the 500-seat theater to the salons and libraries filled with Gobelin tapestries and rare paintings—only with candles.

Maxim's, a new restaurant on Rue Royale, attracted lovers of what was known in French as "*le High Life*," but one did not have to pay Maxim's prices to have a good time in Paris. Baedeker's guide for 1889 advised that three to four dollars a day was enough to enjoy the city "where luxury is raised to a science." If 80 cents was too much for a bottle of champagne, there was always *vin ordinaire* for pennies per liter. A good restaurant dinner could be had for about 30 cents.[6]

Particularly in the imagination of foreigners, Paris at this time was synonymous with a relaxed attitude toward the flesh trade. Actually prostitution in the city was probably no more widespread or flagrant than in London, Vienna or New York, but streetwalkers and *maisons closes* had become a fixed part of the local folklore in a way that they had not elsewhere. Rumor had it that Paris' licensed brothels were frequented by judges and generals, financiers and government officials, foreign princes and visiting VIPs.

Many of the fancier establishments were decorated and furnished with a singular luxury and originality. Some became famous. One such featured rooms in different international styles—a Chinese room, a Russian room, an Italian room, an Indian room, a Persian room, and so on—and another transformed a chamber into the first-class cabin of an ocean liner, the bed suspended so as to imitate the rocking motion of a ship with its occupants' every move. But in reality the number of registered Paris brothels was in decline, having fallen from 145 in 1870 to 73 in 1888.[7]

As the brothel declined, alternative evening entertainment arose in the form of the *cabaret artistique*. Originally semiprivate clubs where small groups of like-minded poets and musicians gathered to sing, play music and recite poetry, cabarets became a fixture of Montmartre nightlife. By the 1890s several had begun to open their doors to the public. They were not for those with tender ears, for the songs and poems ran to Rabelaisian burlesque of bourgeois mores and the mordant political satire of the *chansons rosses*.

One of the earliest and most famous of Montmartre's cabarets was the Chat Noir, which opened in 1881. It had a small stage where authors recited and acted out their compositions, often accompanied by shadow plays on the wall behind. After it was taken over in 1885 by the flamboyant Aristide Bruant—immortalized with a rakish red scarf thrown around his neck in the famous poster by Toulouse-Lautrec—the Chat Noir became a favorite of the *Tout Paris*, which loved to go slumming there even if its fashionable members did not understand the working-class argot used in many of the numbers. Several of the artists who contributed to the Chat Noir's show later became famous, such as Caran d'Ache, who did cutouts for the shadow plays, and playwrights like Alphonse Allais and Maurice Donnay.

"As an artist, a man has no home in Europe save Paris," the German Ubermensch philosopher Friedrich Nietzsche said of this time. The city vibrated like a tuning fork to the world's most stimulating artistic and intellectual community. All rules, concepts and conventions were open to question. The only absolute value was individual perception, imaginatively expressed.[8]

Here *littérature* was something regarded with high seriousness, for throughout the century Paris had been a faithful if exigent muse. The Symbolist poems of Arthur Rimbaud, Paul Verlaine, and Stéphane Mallarmé were quoted in the cafes along with couplets from Edmond Rostand's immensely successful new play, *Cyrano de Bergerac*. Marcel Proust, born with the Third Republic in 1871, published his first work in a magazine, *La Revue Blanche*, in 1889. That same year the young André Gide, as yet unpublished, noted in his *Journal* his vision of the ideal literary life in a garret overlooking the roofs of the Latin Quarter, with "at one's feet, before one's table, Paris. And shutting oneself up in there with the dream of one's masterpiece, and only to come out again with it finished."[9]

But if Gide's youthful longings seen romantic, Romanticism as a literary movement had long since been discredited by the splenetic poems of Charles Baudelaire and the pitiless social observation of Gustave Flaubert, which led to the world-weary short stories of Guy de Maupassant and Emile Zola's harshly naturalistic novels.

It was a great age for the other arts as well. In painting, Georges Seurat and others were recreating the art. Sculpture was receiving new impetus from the powerful work of Auguste Rodin and Aristide Maillol. Literature and the plastic arts had their counterpart in the impressionist music of Claude Debussy, whose horizons had been widened by listening to Javanese orchestras at the Exposition of 1889. On the lighter side, Paris hummed tunes from *Barbe-Bleue*, *La Vie Parisienne* and other popular works of Jacques Offenbach. The city's flourishing theater life was dominated by a skinny, golden-voiced actress named Henriette Bernard, better known as Sarah Bernhardt. And an entirely new art form was born in 1894 when the Lumière brothers made the first short films.

The sciences too blossomed beneath the era's sunny tolerance toward new ideas. Louis Pasteur's monumental work in microbiology—he performed his first audacious inoculation of a human being against hydrophobia in 1885—bolstered the Belle Epoque's assurance that science would eventually conquer all man's ills. It was also during this period that Marie and Pierre Curie, married in 1895, began their studies of radium that would win the Nobel Prize for physics in 1903.

The financial crisis that had hit the country in the mid-1880s was over, and although France's economic development lagged that of the more advanced industrial nations like Britain, Germany and the United States, the Belle Epoque was generally a prosperous period. Nearly half of France's labor force was still engaged in agriculture, but farm income was good and was protected from competition by high tariffs; the rapidly spreading railway network insured easy access to markets.

France had become a front-rank power in trade, the world's largest exporter of iron ore and the third-largest exporter of wheat. It remained the greatest producer of luxury goods such as fine fabrics, perfumes, cosmetics and high-quality wines. Moreover, the increasing national income was untroubled by direct taxation, because the National Assembly voted down proposals for an income tax in 1895 and 1896.

Paris in the nineties was not without its bit of brash Americana, probably best exemplified by James Gordon Bennett. Son of the founder of the New York *Herald*, Bennett was Commodore of the New York Yacht Club and a prominent playboy when he decided to go to Europe in the 1880s after fighting a duel. He soon became a colorful part of the Paris scene, reinforcing his notoriety with such antics as charging up the Champs-Elysées one midnight stark naked at the reins of a coach and four.[10]

In 1887 he founded a Paris edition of the *Herald* as a hobby, reminding the editorial staff that he was the only reader to be pleased. What it pleased Bennett to read in his paper was news of society, weather, ballooning, yachting, ship movements and animals, especially dogs. To keep his friends who summered in Deauville supplied with the paper he loaded copies into a big red Mercedes racing car, which made the 130-mile trip in two and a half hours—nearly as fast as it can legally be made today—leaving a number of upset Norman cows in its wake.

Such was the stuff of Belle Epoque Paris. Like the Eiffel Tower it had engendered, the era was frivolous, but behind the frivolity lay imagination, talent and a high degree of competence. As Barbara Tuchman summed up this grandly ambivalent age in her excellent history, *The Proud Tower*:

> Its inhabitants lived, as compared to a later time, with more self-reliance, more confidence, more hope; greater magnificence, extravagance and elegance; more careless ease, more gaiety, more pleasure in each other's company and conversation, more injustice

and hypocrisy, more misery and want, more sentiment including false sentiment, less sufferance of mediocrity, more dignity in work, more delight in nature, more zest.

But even "the permanent glamour of France," as one English observer described French cachet in the nineties, could not conceal the travail of fin de siècle Paris. Beneath the gaiety and charm ran violent crosscurrents that rent French society with passionate political, economic and religious disputes, while confused moral standards led to public cynicism and corruption on a heroic scale.[11]

By one indirect measure, public confidence appears to have peaked in 1889, for that was the last year the French birth rate exceeded 25 per 1,000; this figure plummeted to 17.5 by 1909. Indeed, the nineties got off to an inauspicious start when Paris was hit, in 1890, by an influenza epidemic, which some French scientists theorized originated in dust compounded of Yellow River mud and the bodies of drowned Chinese, there having been disastrous floods in China in 1888. Paris also experienced an unusually severe winter that year. Crowds of poor flocked to the snow-covered Champ de Mars where temporary shelters were constructed, open fires were kept fueled for warmth, and cauldrons of free soup simmered continuously.[12]

Politically, the Third Republic remained a hazardous balancing act, the result of reluctant agreement among opposing forces to make the best of a bad thing. It had to get along without a constitution, for there was so little consensus at its founding that one could not be formulated; a series of ad hoc constitutional laws formed its legal basis. The threat from the revolutionary Left to France's third experiment in democracy was exceeded only by the determination of the Right to overturn the Republic in favor of a monarchy.

The aristocrats despised the bourgeoisie, which feared the peasantry and the industrial proletariat. The Catholic establishment spurned Protestants, rabid nationalists openly professed their hatred of French Jews. Small wonder then that from its founding in 1871 until 1879, when the Chamber of Deputies and Senate moved back to Paris from Versailles, there were 12 governments, or that there would be 50 by the beginning of the First World War.

Discontent with the bleakness of industrial society and abuses of unbridled capitalism ran high among workers and intellectuals, spawning anarchist terror bombings in cafes, business offices, and the Chamber of Deputies itself from 1892 to 1894. Paris lived in such fear during this period that if a streetcar had minor mechanical trouble or a bit of scenery fell at a crowded theater, panic and cries of "*Les anarchists! Une bombe!*" quickly ensued. In the absence of an Internet, detailed directions for terrorist tactics were listed in pamphlets such as the "Manual of the Perfect Dynamiter."

This wave of terrorism culminated in the assassination of President Sadi Carnot in June 1894, which led to passage of special laws for suppressing anarchist publications and allowing instant searches and arrests of suspects. Carnot's successor, Jean Casimir-Périer, resigned six months later in frustration at the powerlessness of the presidency, and *his* replacement, Félix Faure, lasted only four years before expiring, in perfect fin de siècle style, in a compromising position with his mistress in his office at the Elysée Palace.

Scarcely had the anarchist violence passed when a Jewish army captain named Alfred Dreyfus was unjustly convicted of selling military secrets to Germany, throwing France into one of its worst political convulsions of the century.

Dreyfus, an artillery officer on the French General Staff, was convicted in 1894 by a court-martial held in camera on the basis of fraudulent evidence, and was sent to the inhumane, torturous prison on Devil's Island off the north coast of South America. The army's action was sustained by the atmosphere of virulent anti-Semitism stemming from the French bourgeoisie's fear of Jewish control of the nation's financial life.

French racism was nurtured by hate literature, such as the widely read *La France Juive* by Edouard Drumont, a journalist, published in 1886. Drumont founded the National anti-Semitic League in 1889 to combat "the clandestine and merciless conspiracy" of Jewish finance, and in 1892 started a frankly anti-Semitic newspaper, *La Libre Parole*. But despite Drumont's propaganda and the army's best efforts to close the case, doubts lingered about Dreyfus' guilt. Indeed, no convincing motive could be found for his alleged crime.

The Dreyfus Affair burst on the public consciousness in January 1898, when Emile Zola, then at his height as France's most prestigious author, published an open letter to the President entitled *J'Accuse*, in which he spelled out the arguments against the army's handling of Dreyfus. Public opinion divided sharply along religious and political lines, with Protestants, Jews, freemasons, anticlericals and enemies of the Republic calling for a revision of the judgment on Dreyfus, and the army, Catholics, monarchists and nationalists defending the conviction. Tried and convicted of libeling the army, Zola fled to England, but the tide had turned. Dreyfus was returned from Devil's Island in 1899.

After 12 years, the poisonous affair was finally over when Dreyfus was vindicated by an appeals court in 1906. The episode marked the shameful low point of France's Belle Epoque, which had no lack of other public scandals.

Scandal of Scandals

CUNNING AND CONNIVANCE were the basic components of the tacitly accepted modus operandi of fin de siècle Paris. The highest institutions in the land were besmirched with corruption. In 1887, for instance, the son-in-law of President Jules Grévy was caught trafficking in official decorations from his office in the Elysée Palace, forcing Grévy to resign in disgrace. Three years later, several Paris municipal councilors were involved in murky transactions in municipal bonds, which they had acquired at bargain prices and sold at premium rates.

As a consequence of inadequate banking and financial laws and public gullibility about get-rich-quick schemes, France was wracked by one sensational financial scandal after the other.

One of the first big scandals hit in 1882, when the Union Générale bank suspended payments, resulting in a financial crash that wiped out the savings of thousands of people, including many priests and bishops; the bank had the declared objective of promoting the interests of Catholics, and Pope Leo XIII had himself invested several hundred thousand francs in it. After the collapse, the Austrian ambassador to Paris, Count Wimpffen, who had been implicated in some of the bank's ventures in Austria, shot himself dead in a Paris kiosk. Scandal again resulted in suicide when Denfert Rochereau, president of the Comptoir d'Escompte, killed himself after the bank attempted to corner the copper market and failed.

The financial scandals finally culminated in the most spectacular crash of all. It involved hundreds of thousands of bondholders and compromised nearly 150 members of the National Assembly, dozens of newspapers, several important financial promoters, and the famous builder of the recently completed thousand-foot tower: the Panama Affair.

AS GENERAL CONTRACTOR for the Universal Interoceanic Panama Canal Company since December 1887, Eiffel and Company had plunged ahead with work at a pace that put it well in advance of the schedule called for in its contract with Ferdinand de Lesseps. Steady progress was being made in cutting through the rocky, 400-foot Culebra range. Eiffel's patented canal locks—"a mechanism so simple that a child could set it in motion," he said—were being constructed in Brittany. Lesseps finally having made the decision to build the Panama Canal in the form of a gigantic, 10-lock liquid staircase—Eiffel's idea to begin with—the project seemed to untangle itself for the first time.[1]

But that decision came too late. Not even a great engineering plan could save Lesseps from his naïveté, self-delusion and financial ineptitude.

On December 14, 1888, the Panama Canal Company filed for bankruptcy. It had begun operations eight years before with far less capital than experts had predicted the job would require. Since that time Lesseps and his advisers had consistently and probably deliberately underestimated costs. The company had attempted six public bond issues with diminishing success, the last in December 1888 being less than half subscribed.

Lesseps' promise that "the day will come when Panama stock will stand higher than Suez stock" sounded ever more hollow as Panama bonds fell to a fraction of their original price. A billion and a half francs—nearly $300 million at the time—had vanished into the fever-ridden swamps of Panama. After the National Assembly refused by 256 votes to 181 to prorogate the company's debts, resulting in the declaration of bankruptcy, the Civil Tribunal of Paris officially dissolved the company and appointed a receiver in February 1889, one year before the canal was to be in operation according to Lesseps' optimistic predictions.[2]

At first Eiffel refused to believe that France would allow a project so obviously in its national interest to go under. He ordered work to continue at reduced speed in Panama pending a solution to this latest crisis. After all, the company had struggled from one money problem to another since its beginning, and had always found a way to stagger on. Eiffel did $1.4 million worth more of work under his $25 million contract before being officially advised by Joseph-Mathieu Brunet, the receiver, that there was no hope of being reimbursed for any future expenses he might incur.

Only in the spring of 1889, as the tower was reaching its ultimate height on the Champ de Mars, did Eiffel reluctantly abandon the most ambitious undertaking of his career. He had been betrayed, not by his genius for analyzing an engineering problem and organizing its solution, buy by unscrupulous financial jugglers.

In April Eiffel duly asked Brunet, a former cabinet member and a man of integrity, to settle accounts between his firm and the Panama Canal Company. The two decided that there was no need of a long and costly court procedure. After four months of negotiating they signed an agreement in July 1889, in which both parties declared themselves satisfied and renounced all future claims against each other. The agreement, under which Eiffel as an independent contractor reimbursed the Panama Canal Company $600,000 in advances and turned over all equipment and materiel, was ratified by the Paris Civil Tribunal.

But too much money had been lost, and too much political capital remained to be made, for that to be the end of the Panama Affair. Public opinion, egged on by Edouard Drumont in *La Libre Parole*, pressed for an official investigation of the company's failure. After Drumont attacked Lesseps in his book *La Dernière Bataille* as "this man who has lied so shamelessly, who has abused the public with false promises, who has squandered this money in the most disgraceful way," the National Assembly voted in June 1890 to refer Panama to the minister of justice.[3]

Things moved slowly at first, but in June 1891 the First Chamber of the Court of Appeal appointed an examining magistrate, Henri Prinet, to investigate the management of the Panama Canal

Company's board of directors. Homes and offices of several of the company's officers and Gustave Eiffel were searched and documents seized. Nothing incriminating was found. When Prinet completed his investigation, he recommended against criminal proceedings for lack of evidence of intent to defraud by the company's directors.

But public clamor for the heads of those responsible for the crash increased. Piteous stories circulated of life savings lost, such as the peasant in Bergnac, in southwestern France, who had cashed in his pension, sold his father's watch, and mortgaged land to raise $600 to buy Panama bonds. The enemies of the Third Republic, from Boulangists to royalists and on through the rightist spectrum, were rallying once more in hopes of toppling it.

With this kind of heat on his administration, Prime Minister Emile Loubet ordered his minister of justice, Louis Ricard, to begin prosecutions in the case regardless of what the preliminary investigation showed. On November 21, 1892, the prosecuting attorney indicted Ferdinand and Charles de Lesseps, several promoters, and Gustave Eiffel on charges of swindling and breach of trust.

That same day came the first sign of how far *l'affaire de Panama* would extend across French public life. Jules Delahaye, a Boulangist member of the National Assembly intent upon compromising the government, ascended the speakers' rostrum and stated flatly that some 150 members of the Assembly had accepted payoffs totaling $600,000 to promote the interests of the Panama Canal Company. "There are two categories of Deputies," he charged, "those who took money, those who did not."[4]

"The scandal of scandals in contemporary French history," as a French historian has called the Panama Affair, had burst open. The corruption it revealed in politics, business and publishing shocked even sophisticated levels of public opinion. The scale and diversity of payoffs by the Panama Canal Company to members of the National Assembly and to newspapers to promote its interests, in particular its increasingly unsuccessful bond issues, has perhaps never been equaled, even in France: the company was found to have spent the equivalent at the time of an astounding $4.4 million in bribes.[5]

Suddenly the French language had a new word, *chèquard*, or one who had received payoff checks from the Panama Canal Company. The scandal reached as high as the minister of public works, Charles Baïhaut, and the minister of finance, Maurice Rouvier. And it severely compromised the career of one of the most able French politicians of the age, Georges Clemenceau.

The fact that several of the company's chief promoters were Jews sharpened the public outcry over Panama. When one of them, Baron Jacques de Reinach, died suddenly and possibly by his own hand on November 20, 1892, and another, Cornelius Herz, fled to England, it became clear that they had been playing for very big stakes indeed.

Herz, whose family had moved from France to the United States in 1849 when he was four years old, was a smooth confidence man who had practiced quack medicine, pretended to be an electrical engineer on a par with Edison, and left a trail of bilked victims from New York to San Francisco. In Paris, where he settled in 1877, Herz ingratiated himself with politicians and businessmen, becoming an important shareholder in Clemenceau's newspaper, *La Justice*. In 1886 he was the first American citizen to receive the Grand Cross of the Legion of Honor, thanks to his connections. But after Jacques de Reinach's death, Herz's name was found on two check stubs, each amounting to one million francs. Correspondence in Reinach's possession indicated that he had been blackmailed by Herz, who threatened to reveal the degree of corruption in the Panama Canal Company's operations.

Clemenceau's connection with Herz soon became the best-known secret in Paris, but he was a formidable enemy because of his slashing attacks at the podium, his influential newspaper, and his well-known fondness for settling differences by duel. In December 1892, an ardent nationalist and author of patriotic poems and plays, Paul Déroulède, rose in the Assembly and asked rhetorically who could have been the power behind Herz. "You all know who was this obliging, devoted, indefatigable intermediary, so active, so dangerous," he declared. "His name is on the lips of all of you, but none of you will name him, for you fear three things about him—his sword, his pistol, and his tongue. Well, I shall brave them all, and name him. He is Monsieur Clemenceau."[6]

Clemenceau's answer was to shout, "Monsieur Déroulède, you have lied," and to send his seconds to Déroulède with a demand for a duel. Pistols were chosen for the encounter on December 22, not in the Bois de Boulogne but near the Saint Ouen racetrack north of Paris. Despite Clemenceau's undoubted expertise with arms—during well-publicized practice at a shooting range the day before, he had scored 20 successive bull's eyes—both men were untouched after three shots at 25 paces. Honor was preserved all around, but Clemenceau was driven from public life by the scandal as voters rejected him for the next 10 years. It would be 1906 before "the tiger," as he became known for his vigorous leadership as prime minister during the First World War, would head his first cabinet.

It is an index of the moral tenor of fin de siècle France that when all the investigations were completed, duels fought, trials held and careers compromised, only one man, Baïhaut, was ultimately convicted and sentenced, and then only because he actually confessed to taking a bribe. There was no doubt that the company had seriously mismanaged its affairs and done its best to corrupt politicians and journalists, both of which professions—*plus ça change, plus c'est la même chose*—showed themselves only too ready to be corrupted.

The question concerning Eiffel, however, was whether he should have been implicated at all in the scandal. Public sentiment ran against him because he had made money in Panama. The prosecution's case was that he, along with the board of directors, had misused company funds, and that he had held a position of trust and fiduciary responsibility. He contended that, on the contrary, he had merely signed a contract with the company to execute prescribed engineering services, and had indeed rendered those services in exemplary fashion.

Eiffel engaged one of the best lawyers in France, Pierre Waldeck-Rousseau, a cool, ironic former minister of the interior and future prime minister (1899-1902) to argue his case. Replying in person to the judge's questions concerning his involvement with the Panama Canal Company, Eiffel stated:

> Monsieur Ferdinand de Lesseps called for my help in terms that touched me. Our relationship had been cool since he had founded the company. I had never believed in a sea-level canal, and I was one of the few who voted against it at the meeting in 1879 at the Geographic Society. Monsieur Ferdinand de Lesseps had never forgotten that vote over the years. Still, I had followed the work on the canal closely. When the difficulties of constructing a sea-level canal became generally recognized in 1887, I was visited by Baron de Reinach, who proposed that I enter into negotiations with the company. Oh, I hesitated. I hesitated a long time.[7]

But, Eiffel explained, his sense of duty to the nation compelled him to attempt to save the project. Nonetheless, at the conclusion of the two-week trial in March 1893, the court found Eiffel guilty of misusing funds entrusted to him, while acquitting him of complicity in swindling. He was sentenced to two years in prison and a fine of $4,000. Ferdinand de Lesseps—the "Great Frenchman" to his compatriots—his son and two company promoters were sentenced to five years and $600 fines.

The decision was manifestly unjust to Eiffel, who had never had a hand in managing the company's affairs, and who, as general contractor, actually breathed new life into the operation, albeit too late. Only the highly charged atmosphere in Paris after the scandal broke can explain his indictment and conviction. Fortunately, the Cour de Cassation, France's highest court, kept a cooler head and reversed the decision three months later on appeal.

The court's reasoning did not give entire satisfaction to Eiffel and the other accused, however, since the reversal was based on a statute of limitations technicality; the court did not judge the ultimate question of guilt. In the emotional ambiance of the affair it would have required a Solomon to render justice. Belle Epoque/fin de siècle France, with its perennial problem of political meddling in the affairs of justice, was notably short of men of sure, disinterested judgment.

To the detached observer today, it appears that Eiffel did not fraudulently line his pockets at the investors' expense, although his contract did provide him a normal profit margin. Still, he must have had some notion of what was being done by the company's directors and promoters. If he was culpable to some extent by association, this surely was mitigated by the fact that he, at least, honestly delivered the goods according to his contract.

Eiffel eventually would be vindicated by yet another court. But before that occurred, he had another few yards of post-Panama calvary ahead. The French government still had not given up on the Panama Canal project, and encouraged the receivership to form a new company. The receiver and a government-appointed attorney representing the old company's bondholders, set out to raise $12 million capital to finance the *Compagnie Nouvelle du Canal de Panama*. They hit upon the idea of suing underwriters and contractors who had made money out of the old company, charging them with ill-gotten profits.

After a test case went against one important promoter, banks and underwriting syndicates lined up to buy shares in the new company as fast as they could. The attorney declared that, of the cases against the contractors, the one against Eiffel was the strongest, given the importance of his late role as general contractor. Eiffel got the point and bought $2 million worth of shares in January 1894, thus becoming the new company's largest individual subscriber.

In December of that year Ferdinand de Lesseps, having spent his final six years in semi-comatose senility, died without ever becoming aware of the Panama Affair. As the last gusts of the Panama storm blew through the National Assembly, a deputy raised the question of what the Legion of Honor intended to do about the allegations against one of its illustrious members, Gustave Eiffel. The Legion's Grand Chancellor, General Février, responded by convening a committee of inquiry and summoning Eiffel to testify on his role in Panama.

Results of the inquiry were presented to the Legion's self-regulating body for decision. In a letter dated April 21, 1895, General Février announced to Eiffel: "Considering that an examination of the conduct of Monsieur Eiffel as contractor for work on the Panama Canal shows that he committed no dishonorable act calling for disciplinary measures, the Legion is of the opinion that there is no reason for action against him."[8]

It was becoming more difficult with passing months to get political mileage out of Panama, but the National Assembly made one more endeavor in July, when it passed a motion accusing the Legion of ignoring previous decisions against Eiffel, and inviting the government to reorganize it. Three days later, General Février shot back a stinging reply pointing out that the Legion was not only fully aware of previous cases brought against Eiffel, but also that Eiffel had been declared innocent by the highest court in the land.

Because the entire case was technically invalidated by a statute of limitations, there remained the nagging fact that the Cour de Cassation had not passed on the question of whether Eiffel should have been implicated in his role as independent contractor. But the Legion of Honor had gone into precisely this question, Février emphasized, and found Eiffel innocent of any wrongdoing whatever. He furthermore presented to the President his resignation and that of the 12 other Legion officials, including four generals, a vice admiral, the honorary president of the Cour de Cassation, and several members of the French Academy. The collective resignation was refused.

After five years of calumny, Eiffel was at last officially cleared of the mud of Panama. The canal that would have been his greatest work, easily surpassing in importance and utility all his bridges and the thousand-foot tower, was finally built by American Army engineers, some of whom were vocal in their admiration for what their French predecessors had accomplished. France's New Panama Canal Company sold out to the United States for $40 million in 1904, yielding to the cold geopolitical logic of what President U. S. Grant had called for as early as 1881: "An American canal, on American soil."[9]

Eiffel, reaching for an ever-grander achievement to cap his engineering career, had ignored that logic and the evidence of Lesseps' mismanagement in favor of something that the Belle

Epoque prized more highly—glory. But fate decided that his tower was glory enough.

Career's Creative End

THE MASTER BUILDER would build no more. No matter how unfairly Eiffel had been spattered by the Panama Affair, no matter which tribunal declared his innocence, the stain of scandal could never quite be removed from a rancorous French public opinion. In the wake of Panama, he chose to retire from his company, which later changed its name to the anonymous Ateliers de Construction de Levallois-Perret.

This was a harsh reversal of fortune for Eiffel, but his restless genius demanded outlets. Panama had not demoralized him; retirement would not mean withdrawal. In fact, the next three decades were to be among the most creative of his life, thanks to his imaginative use of the tower as a test bed.[1]

Shortly after the tower was completed, Eiffel made it his laboratory for many kinds of experiments. One of the first things he did was to install thermometers, barometers and anemometers on the third platform in cooperation with France's Central Weather Bureau. The instruments were wired to monitors in the Bureau's offices on nearby Avenue Rapp, and their readings published daily. For the first time, French scientists could compare weather conditions at a 1,000-foot altitude with those directly below at ground level.

Their initial findings seem self-evident today, but caused considerable interest at the time in scientific circles burning with the new empiricist fever: temperatures at that altitude averaged exactly 2.3 degrees centigrade lower than those recorded below; temperature variations were less at altitude than at ground level, and inversions were frequent, especially during September and October; winds were strongest in January and February, and three times as strong above as below. Static electricity in the atmosphere was measured, as was the tower's movement at the top caused by wind and temperature variations—less than five inches' sway in the strongest wind, seven inches' expansion on a hot summer day.

Physiological tests were done to determine the effects of altitude on the human organism. The resulting report provokes a smile today despite its determined effort at scientific solemnity:

> On rising by elevator to the third platform, the respiration becomes more ample and easier; the pulse beats faster, then becomes more regular and hardy. At the same time, the subjects experience a feeling of well-being, of general quickening. The satisfaction of being on a plateau with a vast view of the horizon combines with a particularly vivifying air of great purity to produce, especially in women, a psychic excitement that is translated by gaiety, animated and joyous conversation, laughter, and the irresistible desire to go still higher—in sum, a general excitement which recalls that provoked by visits to mountain resorts. If the stay at the top is prolonged, there is a remarkable sensation of appetite, while the notion of passing time weakens notably.[2]

The physiologist conducting the experiment, who happened to be a son-in-law of Eiffel's, concluded that ascending the tower was excellent therapy for anemia and dyspepsia. But scientific scruples prompt one today to question whether such euphoric results were not due in part to the special nature of the subjects of the experiment—the gay, animated women of the Belle Epoque.

A more serious and fruitful line of experiments, however, was to put Eiffel squarely in the avant-garde of several areas of emerging 20th-century technology, much as his construction techniques with iron represented the forefront of 19th-century civil engineering. His mind as alert at 70 as the day he graduated from Centrale, Eiffel now plunged into basic research in meteorology and aerodynamics, while encouraging the development of wireless telegraphy.

"During my engineering career the wind was always one of my preoccupations due to the exceptional dimensions of my structures," Eiffel explained in his memoirs. "It was an enemy against which I had to struggle constantly. My studies to determine its force led me progressively to investigate other aspects of meteorology, and eventually to set up a complete weather station."[3]

Eiffel's first meteorological observation post was operating on his property at Sèvres, a few miles south of Paris, before the tower was built. He extended his studies to similar stations at his homes on the Riviera and in Brittany, and to the tower in 1889.

Study of weather had made little significant progress since Aristotle had published his *Meteorologica* in the 4th century B.C. When Eiffel suddenly found himself with leisure to devote to the subject, he was dismayed by the obsession of French meteorologists with rigorous but sterile precision, as opposed to creative synthesis. Temperatures were recorded to $\frac{1}{100th}$ of a degree, but were not put into meaningful context.

As a first step toward synoptic meteorology, Eiffel suggested recording only daily minimums and maximums. He also favored putting the figures into graphic form for ready comparison, as was already being done by the United States Weather Service. Appalled as ever by a general lack of system, he found instrumentation woefully lacking in French weather stations, where many observations such as cloud cover, hours of sunshine, and even wind speed and direction were estimated rather than measured.

Eiffel first tackled the problem of instrumentation. He made an effective housing for thermometers and other equipment that gave protection from the elements while permitting a free flow of air. Then he designed improved instruments for observing and automatically recording wind direction and force, insolation and other data. He extended his private weather network to 25 stations, including one in Algiers. Finally, to show the way to a hesitant French Weather Bureau, he published at his own expense a series of weather atlases from 1903 to 1912. These were the first synoptic charts to appear in France, and the foundation of modern meteorology in that country.

Simultaneously, Eiffel kept an interested eye on developments in aviation. At the turn of the century, flying was little more than a sport for tinkerers and playboys. Ballooning was its most popular form, but the fact that balloonists seldom knew where they would land made it a rather unreliable form of transportation.

The tower became involved in aviation when Henri Deutsch, a wealthy French oil man, created a $20,000 prize in 1900 for the first balloon pilot to take off from the landing field in Saint-Cloud, west of Paris, circle the tower 3.4 miles distant, and return within 30 minutes.

The challenge was taken up by Alberto Santos-Dumont, Brazilian-born heir to a coffee fortune, who lived in Paris. Santos-Dumont began building power airships in 1898, and by 1901 he was ready to try the Eiffel Tower run. His first attempt, in July, got him around the tower in 40 minutes — too long to qualify for the prize, but still the first recorded flight of a dirigible around a predetermined course. In August he tried again, but after he cleared the tower, a propeller became fouled in the craft's rigging and it plunged into the Grand Hôtel du Trocadéro across the Seine.

Shaken but unhurt, Santos-Dumont built another dirigible, his sixth, and took off again on October 19. This time he made the round trip in 29 minutes, 30 seconds. The prize was his, along with a commemorative gold medal from the Eiffel Tower Company.[4]

The omen was unmistakable: the tower and its eponymous builder had a role to play in aviation. In 1903, at the age of 71, Eiffel set up a small laboratory on the second platform. While continuing to compile his meteorological atlases, he began a series of separate experiments which, over the next decade, would go far toward putting the fledgling science of aerodynamics on a sound theoretical footing.

Heavier-than-air flying machines were then being built by trial and error out of baling wire and sweat. Steam-powered engines were heavy and unreliable, and no one really knew why a wing, whether on a bird or an aircraft, made flight possible. Early experimenters such as Sir George Cayley in Great Britain had intuitively grasped the nature of powered flight, and outlined the general configuration of aircraft by the mid-19th century. But until the basic laws of aerodynamics were better understood, there could be no systematic advance in aviation.

Eiffel decided that the first question to investigate was the air itself. To find how the resistance of air could be calculated accurately, and what forms moved through the air with least effort, he made use of the unique facility his aerial tower provided to experiment with objects in free fall. Eiffel ran a guide wire from his lab, 377 feet above the Champ de Mars, to a point directly below. Objects of differing profiles could then be dropped, trailing a light wire connected to recording devices in the lab to measure speed. Although the drops lasted only five seconds on average, the objects' speed reached 90 miles per hour.

By 1905, hundreds of tests with round, square, rectangular and triangular plane surfaces had enabled Eiffel to confirm experimentally the generally accepted physical law that air resistance increased as the square of the surface of the object moving through it. Further, the tests showed that the coefficient figure used by many scientists to calculate air resistance—a figure derived from tests in which objects were whirled on turntables rather than moved straight through the air—was off by as much as 56 percent. Confirmed independently by the great American aviation pioneer, Samuel Pierpont Langley, director of the Smithsonian Institution, the new coefficient was Eiffel's first contribution to aerodynamics.

But the drop tests did not entirely satisfy him. To prevent his results from being influenced by wind action, he could conduct experiments only during periods of complete calm. Moreover, the range of test models that lent themselves to this method was severely limited.

Therefore in 1906 Eiffel built a wind tunnel at the foot of the tower. Powered by the tower's generators, a 70-horsepower electric motor drove a fan system that provided a steady, controlled, and turbulence-free flow of air at speeds up to 40 miles per hour through a horizontal test chamber five feet in diameter. Although a number of experimental wind tunnels had been build previously—the first by F. H. Wenham in England in 1871—Eiffel's was the most accurate and soundly conceived by far. Over the next five years this installation became the birthplace of scientific aerodynamics.[5]

Heart of the wind tunnel's equipment was an ultra-sensitive set of scales which, when linked to a model of the airplane being tested, measured its overall aerodynamic balance. Other equipment gave precise readings of lift over wing surfaces and efficiency of propellers. By 1911, Eiffel had carried out over 5,000 experiments with the wind tunnel, enabling constructors to eliminate a good part of the guesswork in designing their prototypes.

In particular, his work led to breakthroughs in two important areas, wings and propellers. As a result of his close study of airfoils, Eiffel proved conclusively that much more lift was produced by the air flowing *over* a cambered wing than by the air striking its underside. Ignorance of this counterintuitive principle by early designers resulted not only in inefficient wing profiles, but also in numerous crashes when canvas was ripped from the tops of wings by the air's suction force during flight.

Propeller design was also made simpler and more effective by Eiffel's discovery that, although propellers might vary greatly in size, they were all essentially similar in their action on the air. They could therefore be designed according to a set equation, which Eiffel drew up in his "Law of Similitude." He also led the way in studying variable pitch and counter-rotating propellers.

With the Champ de Mars neighborhood becoming a favorite residential area of the haute bourgeoisie, complaints began to pour in to city officials about the noisy experiments being carried out at the foot of the Eiffel Tower. The City of Paris informed Eiffel that his wind tunnel violated zoning restrictions, upon which he created another one in suburban Auteuil in 1912.

His second wind tunnel was larger and more powerful than the one at the tower, providing an air flow of 71 miles per hour through a test chamber six and one-half feet in diameter. With it Eiffel continued his experiments on wings at a more realistic airspeed, finding, for example, the best positioning of upper and lower wings on a biplane and their interdependent lift characteristics.

During the following years he studied complete scale models of 17 aircraft. Today their names read like a *Who's Who* of those heroic days of aviation: Wright, Voisin, Blériot, Morane-Saulnier, Bristol, Dorand, Farman, Bréguet, Nieuport among others. Most of the famous Allied fighter planes of the First World War, including the French Spad, were tested at the *Laboratoire Eiffel* before taking to the skies. (The Auteuil laboratory still functions and has been declared a national historical monument by France.

Eiffel adjusts a scale-model airplane in his wind tunnel at Auteuil.

Unsuitable for most aeronautical testing today, it is much used for automobile windstream tests such as Porsche has done there on its sports cars. Stability tests for high-rise structures such as airport control towers, antennas, and offshore drilling platforms are also done, along with wind tests of buildings like the Montreal Olympic Stadium.)

Soon aeronautical engineers in other countries were paying Eiffel the sincerest form of flattery, setting up wind tunnels based on his design in Holland, the United States, and Japan. As always, Eiffel scorned secrecy, freely publishing his methods and results; his voluminous technical study, *The Resistance of the Air and Aviation*, appeared in translation in the United States in 1913.

That same year, the Smithsonian Institution honored Eiffel with America's most prestigious aviation award of the day, the Langley Gold Medal. The first Langley Medal had gone to the Wright brothers in 1910. The second and third were presented to Gustave Eiffel and the American airplane designer Glenn Curtiss on May 6, 1913. The French ambassador in Washington accepted the medal for Eiffel, who could not attend the ceremony.

Alexander Graham Bell, in his capacity as a regent of the Smithsonian, made the presentations. In his speech, Bell noted with some understatement that "The advance has been much greater in the art than in the science of aerodromics." In other words, aviators flew by the seats of the pants rather than improving their craft through an understanding of physical laws. Bell continued:

> This eminent engineer, the constructor of the Eiffel Tower, though more than 80 years of age, still continues his studies in his chosen field of labor with all the enthusiasm of youth, and his writings upon the subject of resistance of the air have already become classical. His researches, published in 1907 and 1911, on the resistance of the air in connection with aviation, are especially important and valuable. They have given engineers the data for designing and constructing flying machines upon sound, scientific principles.[6]

Eiffel still had not exhausted his imaginative use of the tower. While he was conducting his meteorological and aerodynamic studies, his agile mind caught a gleam from yet another technological development that seemed to hold promise for the future.

The tower was a natural communications post, and as early as 1898 Eiffel encouraged the French radio pioneer Eugène Ducretet to perform experiments with a transmitter on the third platform. Ducretet successfully sent radio messages in October of that year to a receiver in the Paris Panthéon, two and a half miles away, "even in thick fog." When he tried reversing the experiment, he was unable to receive on the tower and concluded that the radio signals were being absorbed by the structure's iron beams. Eiffel demurred, pointing out that similar experiments on naval vessels had succeeded despite the ships' enormous metallic mass.[7]

Guglielmo Marconi's experiments in 1899, in which he sent radio waves across the English Channel, proved the worth of wireless telegraphy to all but government bureaucrats. A young captain in the French Corps of Engineers, Gustave Ferrié, was charged with studying ways of adapting the wireless to military use, but the army could offer no financial or technical support. Eiffel wrote the army in 1903 to proffer the tower as Captain Ferrié's laboratory. The army parsimoniously accepted on the condition that it would incur no expenses, so Eiffel undertook to subsidize the work.

The following year Ferrié, working out of a wooden shack and with a single antenna guyed from the tower to a tree on the Champ de Mars, was sending and receiving over distances of 250 miles. By 1908 he had improved his equipment and was reaching Berlin, Algiers, Casablanca and North America; the army, finally convinced, converted the temporary Eiffel Tower station into a permanent facility. In 1911 the station began transmitting Greenwich Mean Time as a navigation aid to ships at sea.

During the First World War Ferrié was a general, and his station paid important military dividends. In August 1914, for instance, the tower's receiver intercepted a radio message from General von der Marwitz, commander of a cavalry division covering the German Army's right flank as it advanced on Paris. Von der Marwitz informed his headquarters that he had run out of feed for his horses and was unable to advance. That helped convince the French General Staff that the time had come to make a decisive counterattack on the Marne—and to requisition a fleet of Paris taxis to transport the French Army there.

Interception of coded messages also led to the French arrest of one Margaretha Geertruida MacLeod, also known as Mata Hari, a Dutch-born dancer who employed her feminine wiles in spying and was executed by firing squad near Paris. A few bloody years later, on November 10, 1918, came the tower's final intercept of the war: "The German High Command accepts the Armistice conditions imposed."

(Following the war, the tower housed France's first civil radio station, broadcasting news and music. Television experiments were performed there in 1925, and in 1953 the country's first TV station began operating from the tower.)

IN 1920, at the age of 88, Gustave Eiffel at last began to slow his pace. He had published 31 books or monographs covering his landmark projects and the results of his scientific experiments. And in his desk drawer he still had plans for challenging, ahead-of-his-time projects: things like a tunnel beneath the English Channel, an astronomical observatory atop the highest mountain in Europe, Mont Blanc, a subway for Paris.

Had he chosen to wear all the honorary decorations awarded him during his career, he would have been bent double beneath a chestful of medals, including the Hungarian Order of Franz-Josef, the Austrian Order of the Iron Crown, the Portuguese Order of the Conception, the Spanish Order of Isabella the Catholic, the Cambodian Royal Order, the Annamite Order of the Dragon, the Italian Order of the Crown, the Russian Order of Saint Anne, the Greek Order of the Savior, the Serbian Order of Saint Sava, and the Japanese Imperial Order of the Rising Sun, besides numerous French citations and the Langley Gold Medal.[8]

But now, as he looked back and began to write his memoirs for his descendants, Eiffel stated unhesitatingly that his greatest work had been the thousand-foot tower, "symbol of force and difficulties overcome." In the twilight of his life he saw it as "this incomparable monument, the tallest ever to come from the hand of man." And he insisted one last time that whatever else it might be, the tower was *beautiful*, even majestic, with that special aura of the colossal that defies ordinary aesthetic principles. As a practical man he was happy that his scientific experiments and the radio station on the tower had proved its utility.[9]

Patriarch of a large, prosperous clan, Eiffel lived with his daughter Claire and her husband, Georges Salles, an engineer and close associate of Eiffel's for many years. He made his home in a palatial town house at the corner of the Avenue Matignon and Rue Rabelais, across from the fashionable Jockey Club in the Champs Elysées district, on the site where, after its demolition, the Time-Life Building was constructed in 1962 (and where this author, by coincidence, had an office for several years). He had purchased the large, elaborate house with a severe façade—some of the family jokingly called it "the ministry"—immediately after his triumph with the tower, but had come to live in it only much later.

Now its sumptuous Second Empire style, with a roomy graveled courtyard to accommodate several automobiles and an imposing stairway leading to an ornate entrance, suited Eiffel's image of himself. There he liked to reign over his five children, their spouses, and his 11 grandchildren at Sunday dinner and family fêtes, the most important of which was on December 15, his birthday. On that day all the grandchildren were expected to present *Bon-papa* with something done by themselves, whether a drawing, or a piano recital, or a recitation in classical Greek. Kindly but aloof, Eiffel was an intimidating presence to the children.

"He was the perfect figure of a grandfather, with his blue eyes, pink cheeks and white goatee," recalled René Le Grain-Eiffel, son of Laure Eiffel and Maurice Le Grain, who was providentially born in 1889 and had a successful career as an automotive engineer. "It would never have occurred to us to try to pull his beard, though, any more than it would have occurred to him to get down on all fours with us. No one ever used the familiar *tu* with him, or for that matter ever saw him in his shirtsleeves." Eiffel remained vigorous physically and mentally well into his 80s, teaching his grandsons to swim and fence. René Le Grain-Eiffel remembers well that terrible December 15 when his little cousin Jacques attempted to fake it through his recitation of a Greek poem, not knowing that *Bon-papa* retained a working grasp of the language from his lycée days.[10]

The times had been good to Eiffel, always a man of his times. He was now immensely wealthy—his company had had an accumulated turnover of more than $14 million by 1890. Besides his Paris town house and his country residence at nearby Sèvres, he owned homes and property in Brittany, Bordeaux, on Lake Geneva, and at Beaulieu-sur-Mer on the French Riviera, where he kept a 90-foot steam yacht. When the humor moved him, he would head for one of these retreats, taking along as many of the family as were free to travel.[11]

Although austere by temperament and upbringing, Eiffel liked his personal belongings to reflect his genteel status. Today his study has been carefully reconstructed by his granddaughter, Henriette Venot, at the country house at Salleboeuf, near Bordeaux. There can be seen his monumental oak desk riddled with secret drawers, bibelots such as a delicate white porcelain pipe with tooled silver cap, a book cover of fine red velvet bearing his initials in silver, an expensive amber cigar holder with "GE" marked in gold, several gilt statuettes of Buddha, paying homage to the French bourgeoisie's turn of the century enthusiasm for chinoiserie. Eiffel's personal library lines the walls: the leather-bound complete works of Voltaire that had belonged to his father, flanked by Hugo, Labiche, Zola, the Goncourts, much of Maupassant but not the offending *La Vie Errante*, whether a deliberate omission one can only surmise.[12]

Eiffel was also world famous, of course, though occasionally he appears to have doubted that his real value was justly appreciated. He was naturally proud of the tower, but then as now that giddy creation often prevented Eiffel's being taken seriously as an engineer and researcher. "I ought to be jealous of the tower," he protested half-seriously. "It is much more famous than I am. People seem to think it is my only work, whereas I have done other things, after all."[13]

At such moments he was glad of even the simplest manifestation of interest in his other work. Le Corbusier once recalled that he had telephoned Eiffel in 1923 to request a photo of the Garabit viaduct to illustrate an article he was writing. The young architect was pleasantly surprised by the receptive amiability of the old gentleman who was reputed to be so distant and crusty: "Eiffel's voice was soft. He was affable, even friendly. He was enchanted by my juvenile admiration."[14]

Eiffel's main work now was writing his memoirs, in reality a brief outline of his life and career intended only for the family archives. In line with the traditional French discretion about family matters, he deliberately refrained from publishing the work, distributing five mimeographed copies to his children after he finished it in September 1923. On December 27 of that year, Gustave Eiffel died peacefully at the age of 91 in his mansion on Rue Rabelais.

Si monumentum requiris, circumspice. That epitaph would be as apt on the Eiffel Tower as it is in Christopher Wren's Saint Paul's Cathedral in London. Indeed, the tower is Eiffel's only proper monument, for contrary to what one might have expected in a city that readily honors its famous sons and daughters with streets and squares bearing their names, Paris officially ignored his passing. No matter that he was one of France's greatest civil engineers since Vauban, who as *ingénieur du roi* under Louis XIV had scattered his tremendous fortifications throughout the realm. No matter that 30 years had passed since the Panama Affair, and Eiffel's being cleared of the miscarriage of justice that had unfairly implicated him. The smear on his name remained in certain ultraconservative circles.

Finally in 1928 a grateful General Ferrié established a private committee to accept contributions for a token memorial to Eiffel. On May 2, 1929, the simple bust of Eiffel by Antoine Bourdelle, a disciple of Rodin's, was unveiled at the foot of the tower's north pier. On its tall plinth the engraved inscription made no mention of his engineering accomplishments, saying only, "Eiffel 1832-1923." There were speeches by Ferrié, the director of Eiffel's alma mater, Centrale, an official of the Ministry of Posts and Telegraph, and the president of the Paris Municipal Council, who praised "the illustrious engineer who endowed the City of Light with a shining beacon."[15]

But not until 1964, on the 75th anniversary of the tower, when the French Ministry of Culture officially made it a national historical monument, did the city consider the question of naming a street for Eiffel. At last on May 5, 1965, a decree was signed naming a portion of an insignificant street running between the Champ de Mars and the tower Avenue Gustave Eiffel. Avenue Eiffel is only about 100 yards long; its principal traffic is strolling tourists. No houses or buildings front it—there will never be a letter addressed to Avenue Eiffel—and few Parisians know of its existence. His country made one last stab at recognizing his importance in the 1990s, when it printed his likeness on the 50-franc bill, just before the franc was eliminated in favor of the euro.

But if France's recognition of the man who gave Paris its world-famous landmark was downright petty as well as too little and too late, it is unfortunately typical of posterity's blinkered view of his achievement. American encyclopedias often omit Eiffel's name in their articles on iron railroad bridges and wind tunnels. A comprehensive book retracing the history of engineering from the beginning of civilization to the present contains no index entries between "Egypt" and "Einstein." Apparently thorough volumes on the history of flight completely overlook his work. Eiffel was right to be jealous of the tower, a creation so prodigious, so insistently present, as to blind the world to a remarkably original engineering career that spanned over half a century of the most jarring technical change in history.

Still, the fault is not entirely the tower's if its builder has remained relatively obscure. Eiffel's habitual self-effacement made it easy to overlook him as just another pragmatic, sober-sided builder and entrepreneur. Victorian discretion and privacy came naturally to him, and he remained for the most part attractively unimpressed by himself. Eiffel's own explanation of his success was typically modest: "From my father I inherited a taste for adventure, from my mother a love of work and responsibility." Clearly this gifted, sensible Burgundian could have done very nearly anything he set his hand to, and done it well—including the making of fine vinegar.[16]

Thirteen

La Grande Dame

AUGUST 25, 1944. In the Eiffel Tower's long, eventful life, marked by all the droll, commercial, and often tragic acts that men of fertile imagination could commit, this day must be considered one of the most significant. Standing slender and graceful in the heart of an embattled Paris, the tower seemed to represent everything that the French had longed for during the German occupation.

To the war-weary men of General Philippe Leclerc's Second Armored Division, it was like a glimpse of the promised land as they sped their tanks and half-tracks toward the city. Paris' lofty symbol had, after all, survived Hitler's threats to reduce it and the city's other monuments to "a pile of ruins." One French tank commander, Captain Georges Buis, later compared sighting the tower to "the Crusaders seeing Jerusalem's walls." And two drivers of half-tracks ended with a mad race through Paris beneath the tower's arches — with a dinner at Maxim's to the winner — mindless of whether the structure had been mined by retreating German, as many Parisians were convinced. (It had not.)

While Allied Shermans and German Panzers jousted in clouds of acrid smoke on Place de la Concorde, the tower was the scene of one of the most evocative vignettes of the Liberation, perhaps the ultimate popular gesture proclaiming the city's regained freedom.[1]

One man in particular had waited impatiently for this moment. Lucien Sarniguet, a 45-year-old captain in the Paris fire department, had had the duty of lowering the French flag from the tower's mast for the last time on the morning of June 13, 1940. At that time he had vowed to himself to be the first to raise the tricolor when the German occupation ended. Now, having eagerly followed, through the clandestine radio broadcasts of the Resistance, the advance of Leclerc's Second Armored, Sarniguet judged that

August 25 would be crucial in the battle for Paris. He intended to boost French morale the best way he knew.

At noon he arrived at the foot of the Eiffel Tower, accompanied by three men from his detachment carrying a heavy, tattered package tied with a length of laundry rope. In the package was a flag Sarniguet himself had made a few days earlier from old bed sheets and weak wartime dyes of red and blue. He and his men began the ascent of the 1,671 steps, despite the battle that raged around the École Militaire, where a German unit was making a determined last stand. When the Germans saw Sarniguet's group climbing the stairs they opened fire on them, sending bullets ricocheting through the tower's iron beams.

But what Sarniguet saw above him was worse, in a very personal sense, than the danger from German rifle fire: two other men were already halfway up the stairs with a flag in their arms. He bounded up the steps three at a time, but could not catch the others, personnel from the nearby French Naval Museum. Trembling with fatigue and frustration just below the top, Sarniguet watched as the two raised the French flag on the Eiffel Tower for the first time in four years. Then, suddenly forgetting his disappointment, he found himself grinning and hugging the men who had beat him to the top—the occupation was over, as every Parisian knew who saw the tricolor snapping that afternoon atop the tower.[2]

The tower had suffered humiliation along with Paris' citizens during the war. The German Army had quickly seized the Eiffel Tower on June 14, 1940, only weeks after its blitzkrieg offensive broke through French defenses in the Ardennes. French radio operators just managed to destroy the tower's valuable transmission equipment before the Nazis took over and affixed a giant white *V* for victory above the second platform. But the German occupiers did not dare carry out rumored plans to cut up the structure for scrap in 1942, sensing that the population's reaction would turn toward outright revolt.[3]

Occupation troops on leave made the tower a popular tourist attraction once again—some 15,000 per day made the ascent during the summer of 1940—despite having to walk up. The French Army had ordered the tower's director, Etienne Marc, to destroy completely the elevator systems at the same time the radio equipment was wrecked. But Marc could not bring himself to smash the cabins, pulleys, pumps and the rest. Instead, he cut the cables and put several electric switches and motors out of commission.[4]

This did not deter the Germans from installing a radio station at the top, but it was most unfortunate in view of the Führer's visit to Paris the following winter. Adolf Hitler, it was said, felt a personal association with the tower—he was born in 1889—but the nonfunctioning elevators spoiled his tour of it and thwarted his ambition to view Paris, gem of his Thousand Year Reich, spread supine at his feet. He refused to climb the tower's stairs, settling instead for having himself photographed, like any tourist, as he stood on the terrace of the Palais de Chaillot with the tower as backdrop.

The occupation authorities forbade anyone but Germans on the tower. The soldiers continued to visit it in droves, paying only a symbolic one-franc admission, compared with the prewar price of 10 francs. Immediately after the Liberation, American Signal Corps troops climbed up and established their radio post on the third platform, securing communications with the Channel ports, Britain, and American and French troops operating east and southeast of Paris. (Later, Major General H. C. Ingles, Chief Signal Officer of the War Department, wrote Eiffel's grandson, Robert Salles, to thank him for use of the tower, which had been "of the greatest value to the American and French Forces.")[5]

Marc went to work on the elevators as GIs and Parisians began streaming up the stairs in the summer of 1945. Cables and electrical systems had been replaced by June 1 of the following year. Boisterous American troops proved a mixed blessing to the tower. They rendered the service of scratching out the "Fritz, Munich" inscriptions on the tower's wooden handrails and replacing them with the eminently more desirable "Ed, Brooklyn" variety. But the Yanks did show an alarming propensity for tossing empty champagne bottles from the second-platform nightclub. Too happy to dampen the celebrations, the tower's management simply took out special insurance against injury to pedestrians below.[6]

Hitler poses before the tower during his visit to Paris: next best thing to being on it.
(Photo Bibl. Nat. Paris)

THE WAR OVER, the tower not only resumed its place as Paris' foremost tourist sight, but also began the steep climb in attendance figures that was to make it one of the most visited paying monuments in the world. After drawing nearly 2 million paying visitors during the Exposition of 1889, the tower had declined in popularity until the 1900 Paris World's Fair, when a few over 1 million ascended it. (Having replaced the noisy elevators in the east and west piers with smoother hydraulic units and strung 5,000 electric lights from top to bottom, Eiffel was disappointed in the 1900 figure; but that year the centers of attraction were the Grand Palais and the Petit Palais near the Champs Elysées, a discouragingly long walk from the tower.)

Visitors dropped to an all-time low of 121,144 in 1902 and hovered around 200,000 annually until the First World War. The tower was closed to the public from 1915 through 1918, but thereafter it averaged better than half a million visitors until war again closed it in 1940. In 1947 the million mark was passed for the first time since 1900. With postwar prosperity creating world tourism and the tower an obligatory stop on even the most cursory visit to Paris, the figures accelerated steadily: 1.5 million in 1956, 2 million in 1963—the first time the record of 1889 was bettered—and now averages over 6 million yearly. To date, over 200 million people have visited the tower since its creation.[7]

Year in, year out, *la Grande Dame du Champ de Mars*, as the French media invariably call it, when it is not *la Dame de fer*, is the most visited paying monument in France, easily topping the Arch of Triumph, Notre Dame Cathedral, the châteaux of the Loire Valley, and Mont-Saint-Michel. It also outdraws comparable attractions in the United States such as the Washington Monument and Statue of Liberty.[8]

The tower's magnetic appeal prompted one French newspaper columnist to remark that a *touriste* was by definition someone who came to Paris to visit *la Tour*. Three-quarters of the "towerists" are foreign, and of those a majority are American. When the number of American tourists in Paris dropped post–September 11, 2001, the tower felt it immediately, with admissions dropping several percentage points from previous years.

Those clicking turnstiles at the tower's feet are music to the ears of it owner, the City of Paris. Managed by a private company, the Société Nouvelle d'Exploitation de la Tour Eiffel (SNTE), the tower generates a turnover of some $50 million annually, including admissions, concessions for several restaurants, and rental of its 116 antennas—which now bring its total height to 318 meters, or 1,043 feet—by six television channels and 28 FM radio stations. That makes it the only Paris monument to actually turn a profit. The company employs around 250 personnel, from supervisory engineers to technicians and those operating the elevators, selling tickets and patrolling the platforms.[9]

Ownership of the tower is a complex affair in the French manner, involving the public sector—the City of Paris—and private sector, including the SNTE and other private financial partners. This led to near-disaster for French pride in 1999, when one of the private partners was almost sold to a wealthy Texan. "This put the mayor of Paris into a cold sweat," explained the unabashedly chauvinistic *Le Figaro*, for it would have meant that "the tower could have fallen into American hands, a public insult that *la Dame de fer* was ultimately able to avoid." Insulting indeed.[10]

THE TOWER'S BIGGEST single maintenance job is painting it, or "giving her a new dress," as Parisians inevitably like to put it, every five years from the first platform to the top, every 10 from the ground to the first level. A contractor brings in a small, agile army of 25 painters. (Local legend has it that only celibates are accepted for this hazardous job, but that is a bit of harmless Paris folklore; the contractor simply pays a higher insurance premium on his married workers.) They scrub off accumulated grime, touch up rusty spots with red lead, then lay on one thick coat—about 60 tons—of a rust-inhibiting silicone and lead paint. Besides possessing special protective qualities, the paint has to be elastic enough not to crack when the tower sways, expands and contracts.[11]

All painting must be done by brush, since spray guns would put more paint in the air than on the tower's 15,000 structural members. On a windy day, even careful brush work results in complaints from pedestrians, motorists, and apartment dwellers in the vicinity of the Champ de Mars who are struck by airborne droplets carried hundreds of yards. To avoid the summer's tourists and winter's rigors, painting can be done only in the spring and fall, so the $3.7 million job usually takes two calendar years to complete.

The tower's color has evolved from the original reddish brown to chocolate brown to today's indefinable gray beige, or *ton Tour Eiffel*, as the contractor labels it. The aesthetic technique has remained the same: a darker tone from the ground to the first platform, a slightly lighter one from there to the second level, and a still lighter one from there to the top, to accentuate the impression of height. But lively arguments have marked the decision on exactly what color to make the city's symbol.

One of the more colorful debates occurred in 1968, when the writer André Malraux as minister of culture lobbied whimsically for a green Eiffel Tower, while the prefect of Paris wanted blue-gray, "like the Paris sky." Concerned officials suggested, in all, 15 colors that year, ranging from a somber dark gray to lively pink and azure blue. Newspapers entered the fray, one editorially plumping for a patriotic tricolor tower resplendent in tones of *bleu-blanc-rouge*. The tower's managers diplomatically sidestepped the wilder ideas. After everyone had had his fun, the company quietly ordered the contractor to go ahead with the discreet gray-beige they had wanted all along, feeling this color sets off the tower subtly but effectively against the sky.[12]

Occasionally, Paris thrills to rumors about the supposedly parlous condition of the Eiffel Tower. As noted earlier, it was predicted that it would fall during its construction. In 1909, the work was that since Eiffel's 20-year lease was up, the tower would have to be dismantled and move elsewhere, or simply scrapped. While implausible, the idea was not beyond the pale of possibility.

Uncertainty over the tower's future after the turn of the century spurred Eiffel to establish more firmly its utilitarian role; his invitation to General Ferrié to make use of the tower as a military communications post, for example, was in large part enlightened self-interest.

French media fan the slightest ember of speculation about the tower's imminent demise. Even the solemn *Le Monde* succumbed some years ago and asked in a scare headline, "Will the Eiffel Tower Have To Be Razed?" The structure was in such bad shape, the paper reported, that necessary repairs would cost twice the expense of simply tearing it down. Next day, presumably anxious Parisians were reassured by the same paper that "The Eiffel Tower Is in Good Health." All it needed was partial replacement of some columns, which in fact was already being done.[13]

But by 1979, the *Grande Dame* was seriously showing her age. A blue-ribbon technical committee found that its 90-year-old girders were twisting under the excess weight of a heavy concrete floor and other additions on the first platform that had been made over the decades. Its ancient elevator to the top was unusable part of the year, overall safety was found to be poor, and maintenance shoddy. This time, catastrophe was a real possibility. Jacques Chirac, then mayor of Paris, decreed that the tower would be restored before its centennial in 1989.

When the $39 million renovation began in March 1981, the first task was to remove the first platform's heavy concrete floor. That entailed building a temporary platform beneath it, and then dismantling the original platform, ridding it of its excess weight, and rebuilding it with lighter materials. This saved some 1,343 tons, bringing the structure's weight back to the initial 9,700 tons. That allowed the addition of new boutiques, snack bars, souvenir stands, video museum, conference room, and post office with an official "Paris Tour Eiffel" postmark, all intended to prompt visitors to stay longer than the half-hour of the average visit, and spend more than the usual $8.

At the same time, workers straightened the twisted girders beneath the platform with powerful jacks. Safety was improved with fire detectors and sprinklers, as well as by eliminating gas ranges from the restaurant kitchen, making them all-electric. Workers removed the ornate old restaurant on the second level (it was sold to an American restaurateur in New Orleans), and replaced the wobbly 978-step spiral staircase to the top—auctioned off to souvenir hunters—with two straight flights of stairs.

Then there was the problem of the aged Otis hydraulic elevator to the top. It could not be used in winter due to the danger of its water freezing, and it still required an inconvenient change of cabins halfway up. Otis France designed a $2.3 million computer-controlled system of elevators powered by 100-kilowatt electric, gearless motors, the biggest in Europe at the time. The firm installed four new, bright yellow and red elevator cabins straight up through the tower's center. Rising at six feet per second, with a capacity of 1,600 persons per hour, compared with 600 per hour before, the new elevators shortened waiting lines considerably.

With safety and convenience improved, the tower's evening appearance was spruced up. Its illumination at night had gone from hundreds of primitive light bulbs when it was inaugurated, to 1,290 ordinary spotlights positioned around it below. But, like the wind, most of their light passed through the girders and was wasted, and they gave it a cold, spectral appearance against the night sky.

A specialist at lighting châteaux in the Loire Valley for their *son et lumière* shows on summer evenings, Pierre Bideau, had a better idea. He would light the tower from the *inside*. He mounted high-pressure sodium lamps ranging from 150 to 2,000 watts within the girders themselves, 336 of them from top to bottom. The stunning result is a golden shaft of even, height-enhancing light all over.[14]

⚭

THE TOWER's jewel-like lighting today recalls the time when it served as the biggest illuminated advertising sign ever built. That occurred in 1925, when André Citroën rented space on the tower to advertise his automobiles.

Tower management had been looking for a way to liven up the structure on the occasion of Paris' great *Arts Décoratifs* exposi-

The tower's illumination today.

tion that year, which was held nearby. One proposal called for a project on a suitably gigantic scale: the tower would become an immense torch composed of flaming arabesques that turned into stars, shooting comets and animated sighs of the zodiac. Tower officials liked the idea, but balked at the price of half a million dollars. Citroën heard of the project and agreed to finance it in return for the right to put his name in lights on the tower in letters 98 feet high along with the company's chevron symbol. The deal was done.

One can only conjecture what Gustave Eiffel would have thought of turning his tower into a luminous billboard outshining even the most outlandish examples of Times Square Art, but he would likely have admired the engineering prowess it entailed. First, a generating station with a 1,200-watt capacity was installed at the foot of the tower to power 250,000 lights of six colors. From there ran a column of 32 electrical cables, each as thick as a man's wrist. The installation required 375 miles of wiring, the whole carefully camouflaged within the structure. Besides animated figures and the Citroën name, which ran from the second platform to the top on the three sides facing the center of Paris, pearly strings of lights outlined the tower's arches and lower piers.

The tower went up in its artificial blaze for the first time on July 4, 1925. Each flash of animation lasted five seconds, followed by 40 seconds of total illumination and 40 more of the Citroën logo, all visible from 24 miles away. Little criticism of the commercialism of the operation was voiced, and in succeeding years it was extended and refined. In 1926, another 125,000 bulbs and 420 miles of wiring were added to create the illusion of cascades of colored water and luminous fountains. In 1927, lightning zigzagged down the tower and it burst into flame, thunderstruck by an additional 4,000 bulbs.[15]

Commercial or not, the Citroën gimmick was a welcome sight on May 21 of that year to a lone American aviator searching for luminous reference points below as he completed the first trans-Atlantic flight, New York to Paris. Charles Lindbergh later recalled in detail his arrival over the city at 9:52 P.M. and his aerial salute to the tower:

I'm still flying at 4,000 feet when I see it, that scarcely perceptible glow, as though the moon had rushed ahead of schedule. Paris is rising over the edge of the earth. It's almost 33 hours from my take-off on Long Island. As minutes pass, myriad pinpoints of light emerge, a patch of starlit earth under a starlit sky—the lamps of Paris—straight lines of lights, curving lines of lights, squares of lights, black spaces in between. Gradually avenues, parks and buildings take outline form; and there, far below, a little offset from the center, is a column of lights pointing upward, changing angles as I fly—the Eiffel Tower. I circle once above it, and turn northeastward toward Le Bourget.[16]

The world's biggest clock, with a face 50 feet in diameter, was the new twist in 1933; the "hands," actually spokes of multicolored lights, operated sequentially to show the hour and minute. (This was the second time the tower had been turned into a Brobdingnagian clock; the first was in 1907, when luminous numerals 20 feet high flashed the hour from the second platform.)

The last pre-war light trick on the tower, in 1934, was to install 1,000 more lights and 15 miles of cable to create a thermometer that reached from the second level to the top. White lights outlined numerals from zero to 30 degrees centigrade, and formed the thermometer's spine. As the temperature rose or fell, a parallel line of red lights—the "mercury"—crept up or down; the distance between degrees was eight feet.

Citroën discontinued his sign, which cost nearly $120,000 a year to operate, at the end of 1936. Since then nothing has been created to compare with it and probably never will be, given the more critical cast of public opinion toward such garish promotion gimmicks. Another French automobile maker, Peugeot, wanted to rent space on the tower in 1968 for a much more discreet sign to promote a new model, but the Paris Municipal Council rejected the bid for aesthetic reasons. The last time the tower really blazed with light was during the Paris World's Fair of 1937, when six miles of fluorescent tubes outlined its curving edges, and every evening a gigantic display of pyrotechnics shot fountains of fire from the first and second platforms, long colored tracers arching out in all directions.

By comparison, even the 20,000 flashing lights that made the tower glitter and sparkle on January 1, 2000 — travel agents touted the tower, where an electronic clock counted down the century's last days, hours, minutes and seconds, as one of the must places to be on that notable New Year's Eve, along with Egypt's Pyramids and New York's Times Square — seem relatively tame. They generated the predictable oohing and aahing that evening, however, and after they were turned off 18 months later, Parisians and tourists were dismayed. Tower management got the point and spent nearly $5.5 million to have them reinstalled in early 2003, when they began flashing like strobe lights on the hour for 10 minutes in the evening.[17]

But it was also back in 1937 that the quaint, Belle Epoque arcades were removed from the first platform to give the tower a more severely modern, rectangular appearance. The transformation was unfortunate in the opinion of those who liked the tower with all its quirky originality. But in becoming darker and duller in the late 1930s, the tower once again faithfully reflected its era: an age of gentle nonsense was fast drawing to a close as the lights, in the statesman's phrase about an earlier period, began going out all over Europe.

Comedy and Tragedy

OF HUMAN NONSENSE, foolishness and pathos the tower has seen more than its share. Like every unconventional object of significance these days, it seems to serve as a lightning rod for the race's more erratic impulses.

Many of the zanier activities associated with the tower have had at least a pretense of serious endeavor, such as Santos- Dumont's dirigible flights and, in 1909, Compte de Lambert's daring flight over the top of it in a flimsy Wright biplane. But well before then, the tower had begun to attract showoffs and oddballs.[1]

As early as 1891, a Paris baker named Silvain Dornon found brief fame by wobbling up the 363 steps to the first platform on a pair of stilts.[2] A Paris sports daily sponsored a foot race up the tower in 1906 which attracted 120 starters; the winner made it to the first platform in three minutes, four seconds, a robust lady named Madame Boude finished in eight minutes, and a more ambitious contestant charged up the 744 steps to the second platform in the same time with 100 pounds of cement on his shoulders.[3]

In the land of the Tour de France, the bicycle naturally had its place on the tower. In 1923 someone tried the first stunt with a *vélo*. In June of that year a Paris sports writer, Pierre Labric, took a warm-up turn around the first platform on his bike and then headed for the stairs. He bumped down to the cheers of a band of cronies and rubberneckers in record time — necessarily a record, whatever it was, since he was the first. The world seemed to feel he was welcome to it, no one challenging it until 1958, when a stunt man from Saint Tropez named Coin-Coin went Labric one better by negotiating the staircase on a unicycle.[4]

But there's no stopping progress, and a mountain bike allowed a French cyclist named Hugues Richard to make it up to the second platform on his fat-tire bike in only 19 minutes and four seconds in April 2002.[5] It is a moot point with tower buffs as to whether Coin-Coin, Labric, and Richard were not all bettered by Gilbert Dutrieux, a 39-year-old Parisian who in 1959 went up with no wheels at all, but only one leg.[6]

Depression and war dampened the imagination of Eiffel Tower nuts, but a few days after the Allies took Paris, it is said, a B-17 Flying Fortress of the U. S. Army Air Corps zoomed deftly between the tower's legs. That was the first time a pilot had attempted the feat since a 23-year-old Frenchman, Léon Collot, tried it in a light plane in November 1926. Collot's elder brother lived on the Champ de Mars, and Léon wanted to give him a thrill by buzzing the tower at grasstop level. He lined up his plane with the Trocadéro across the Seine, headed in over the Iéna Bridge, and was doing well until the morning sun, rising behind the École Militaire, caught him square in the eyes. Blinded momentarily, he veered slight to the left, caught a wing in one of the antenna cables strung from the tower, and crashed in flames on the Champ de Mars. Of the hundreds of fatalities associated with the tower, Collot's was the most tragically spectacular.[7]

Aviators continue to be tempted by the tower's wide arches, though fortunately few go through with it. Another one who did was an ex-Marine pilot named Robert Moriarty, who had flown 824 missions in Vietnam. On the morning of March 31, 1984, he aimed a Beechcraft Bonanza down the Champ de Mars and passed between the tower's pillars. Asked by an inquiring French reporter why he did it, he gave a typically American reply that was surely incomprehensible to typical Frenchmen: "Just for fun." (Alas for the image of Gay Paree, neither the word nor the concept "fun" exists in French.)[8]

For a while, adventurers — to use the most charitable term — expressed themselves on the Eiffel Tower as if it were an iron mountain. The fad began on a July evening in 1954, when a 22-year-old German student shinnied up through the crossbraces. Around midnight he reached a point above the second platform and settled down on a beam to sleep, waking in time to reach the top by nine the next morning. When he got there he was welcomed by the police, who hustled him to the local *commissariat* for questioning and then released him.[9]

What had seemed a bit of silliness at the time was consecrated 10 years later, when it was included in the official celebration of the tower's 75th anniversary. As part of the festivities in May 1964, four experienced mountain climbers traded their crampons for tennis shoes and charged up the trusswork of the west pier. As Eurovision hookups to 14 countries allowed some 50 million viewers to follow the action on their television screens, the alpinists clambered by amused tourists on the first platform, belayed past the overhang at the second level, and followed their Italian leader up the nearly vertical ascent to the crest.[10]

At one point it appeared the group might be upstaged by a lone climber in a business suit and street shoes who reached the first platform faster than the professionals. He was a Hungarian house painter who knew the tower well from having painted it, but was intercepted by police at the first level and the show went on. The Italian made a crowd-pleasing rappel straight down through the tower's center, while his companions, their work finished for the day, took the elevators down.

Except for a Norman cow named Kilkee that was hoisted up in 1968 to promote dairy products, most of the more lighthearted attacks on the Eiffel Tower's dignity have had an athletic angle of some sort. Others, including a well-organized group of five French students, scaled it, and at least one person, Alan Hackett of New Zealand in 1987, bungee jumped from the second level, plunging to within eight feet from the ground and yo-yoing on his rubber cord half a dozen times.[11]

Arnold Palmer drove a golf ball off the second level in 1977, getting extra hang-time. Philippe Petit, the tightrope walker who made it between New York's Twin Towers on a wire, walked one for nearly 800 yards from the Trocadéro across the Seine to the tower's second level to celebrate its centenary in 1989.[12] At one point there was a hare-brained project to erect a plastic ski slope from the first platform to the ground. Parisians would slalom down the

600-foot slope and end up in a simulacrum of an Alpine village complete with chalets and skating rink. But the Eiffel Slope never got off the ground for lack of financing.[13]

Modern day protesters have used the tower as the means to their diverse ends, political or otherwise. A group of Cubans hung a 20-foot black-and-red flag from the first platform in 1958 to promote Fidel Castro's revolutionary 26 of July movement and decry the sixth anniversary of Batista's coup d'etat. During Vice President Hubert Humphrey's tumultuous official visit to Paris in April 1967, demonstrators against the Vietnam War strung a giant if unimaginative "U. S. Go Home" banner on it. And one irate citizen chose the tower in January 1968 as the ideal spot from which to protest what he considered the poor quality of television programs on French state television, for which citizens pay a hefty tax: he hauled his TV set up to the first platform and threw it off.

ON THE WHOLE, though, it seems to be not the lighter but the darker side of an unbalanced human psyche that responds most often to the tower. On an August evening two years after it was built, a demented printer's assistant gravely climbed 50 feet up the north pier, lighting his way with the butts of three candles. He undressed, left a note willing his clothes to Gustave Eiffel, and carefully hanged himself.[14]

His was the first of several hundred suicides on the Eiffel Tower. (No official count of suicides on the tower has ever been kept.) The tower probably cannot claim a world's record in this grim field, for San Francisco's Golden Gate Bridge, located in the city with one of the highest suicide rates in the United States, has been the jumping-off place for hundreds of suicides since its construction in 1937. But more despondent persons have chosen it for their last act than any other place in Paris, including the bridges on the Seine. Only a few dozen known suicides have been committed, for instance, from the towers of Notre Dame Cathedral.

Perhaps the *douceur de vivre* of the Belle Epoque precluded such ghastly gestures. Whatever the reason, no one leaped to his death from the tower until 1911, after it had been a fixture in Paris for 22 years. Even then, the leap was on the pretext of a scientific experiment.

A tailor named Teichelt had made a spring-loaded bat-wing cape which, he contended, would enable him to fly. Perhaps having heard that earlier in the year an inventor had successfully jumped from the first platform to test a parachute for aviators, Teichelt requested permission to do the same with his cape. With considerable trepidation, the Eiffel Tower Company acceded to his request on condition that he also obtain police authorization and sign a waiver clearing the company of any responsibility in the event of an accident.

He complied and showed up with a handful of well-wishers at 8 o'clock on an exceptionally cold December morning. Press photographers were on hand as well. Once on the ledge of the first platform, Teichelt's courage faltered, but goaded by taunts from excited spectators and blasé photographers he finally stepped timidly over the edge. His complicated cape fluttering uselessly, the poor man assumed the aerodynamic characteristics of a rock. The hole he dug in the frosty earth beneath the tower was nearly a foot deep.[15]

The grisly precedent had been set. Barely eight months later a young woman rode up to the top, calmly mounted a stool to reach the narrow, chest-high observation window, squeezed through, and landed in pieces on the second level. She literally had been cut in two when she struck a crossbeam on the way down.

Since then the Eiffel Tower has witnessed the despair of a cross-section of humanity: from a schoolboy of 15 apparently depressed by bad grades, to a young actress who felt she had failed in the theater, to a wealthy playboy, to a man of 75 with an incurable disease — the tower has been both their way out of an unendurable impasse and a final, dramatic refusal of anonymity.[16]

Most suicides have been French, but many have been foreign, some coming to Paris for the express purpose of jumping from the tower. Periodically there were public outcries for anti-suicide measures, but tower management at the time was reluctant to put up extra-high guardrails for fear of impairing the view and giving the tower a sinister, besieged appearance. Besides, it was argued, if a person cannot commit suicide on the Eiffel Tower, he will simply choose the nearby Seine or another method.

There was, for example, the case of a middle-aged man who had hopped over the railing of the first level and at the last minute was prevented from falling by a tower guard who caught his leg. Hauled back, he was taken to one of the restaurants on the structure and given a free lunch to cheer him up. He admitted he could think of no valid reason to commit suicide, and, apparently fully recovered from his fit of depression, happily offered to buy champagne for his hosts. To insure that he made it home all right, a tower employee drove him to his house in the suburbs. The next morning, he was found drowned, lying face down in one of the small duck ponds at the foot of the tower. He was only one of several such incorrigibles who subsequently killed themselves after being saved on the tower.[17]

On the other hand, increased prevention obviously can save lives. As an example of how little is sometimes necessary, the story is told of a man who had come to the tower with the intention of committing suicide, but had changed his mind when he missed the elevator. He decided not to wait for the next one, went home, and wrote a letter to tower management telling of the incident and enclosing a handsome tip for the elevator operator who had unwittingly saved his life.[18]

There have been other happy endings. One day a young woman jumped from the first level but became entangled in the trusswork and was retrieved, unharmed, by firemen; a few months later she gave birth to a healthy baby boy. Another woman leaped from the first platform and landed on the pliant roof of a little Renault Dauphine, escaping with only a ruptured spleen.[19]

The worst acceleration of suicides was in the early 1960s. Fatal leaps were averaging one per month, sometimes occurring within 24 hours of each other, as sensational media coverage encouraged a snowball effect. One day it was a woman of 41, the next day a man of 33, who managed to shake lose when a guard attempted to hold him back by his coattails. A month later a woman of 50 jumped from the second platform, bounced twice on the west pier, and crashed through the awing of the restaurant on the first level. Paris municipal counselors urgently demanded that the city authorities find a way to stop what had become a suicide epidemic.

The Paris prefect studied possible solutions, from a grille around each platform, to plate-glass mirrors above existing handrails, or nets beneath each platform to catch jumpers. He rejected them all because, as he said, "They would be ugly or ineffective or dangerous for the stability of the tower due to greater wind resistance. Besides, if people cannot jump from the platforms, they can still jump from the stairs, and we can't put a guard on every step."[20]

But public pressure increased, and murder on the tower was added to its already catastrophic suicide record when a Spaniard pushed his wife from the second platform while pretending to hold her back from jumping. For a while, the top was blocked to the public as a preventive measure—and the first day it was closed, a 60-year-old man was just barely stopped by a guard on the second level as he swung a leg over the edge.

Finally in 1965 the prefect ordered the tower to put up a five-and-one-half-foot steel wire fence around each platform. But determined suicides easily managed to scale the fences. Nine months and 12 deaths later, tower management heightened the barriers to 10 feet, with a backward overhang on the second level to make it still more difficult to get over. The observation platform at the top was completely caged in. Today several persons a year, French and non-French, continue to evade patrolling guards, negotiate the barriers, and leap to their deaths.

Besides involuntarily becoming a notorious suicide spot, the tower has had other troubles. First it was announced that the structure would be moved a few yards so as to span the Seine—two feet on the Left Bank and two on the Right—with the Iéna Bridge running beneath. Some time later came the news that the tower was to be loaned to Greece as a goodwill gesture. The plan was to dismantle it and place the pieces in hatboxes specially designed by a Paris couturier. As it happened, both announcements occurred on the first of April of different years, and both were April Fools' jokes perpetrated respectively by the French television network and a Paris newspaper. Further evidence that French wit isn't what it used to be.[21]

But the fire that destroyed the television relay station and weather bureau facilities atop the tower in January 1956 was real enough. When firemen arrived they found that only a few gallons of water were available for their hoses, and watched helplessly as intense heat destroyed 80 tons of equipment and popped rivets in the iron beams of the top platform. The entire supporting structure at the top was deformed and had to be rebuilt, while half of Paris went for months without its ration of TV programs. Fortunately the wooden walls of Gustave Eiffel's private studio, which has been preserved as he left it, had been replaced by iron the month before, saving it from destruction.[22]

Fire has broken out at the tower several other times, mostly relatively insignificant incidents such as a kitchen fire in a restaurant in 1998, and a safety net that caught fire in 2000. But the smoke and flames that engulfed the top one evening in July 2003 created much more alarm. Parisians' nerves were already on edge after months of periodic, post-9/11 terrorist threats, so when thick white smoke and orange flames could be seen at the top of the Eiffel Tower, the worst was feared. It was not a terrorist bomb, however, but a banal electrical short circuit in an equipment room that sent 20 fire trucks howling to the Champ de Mars with 125 firefighters.

They were able to take the elevators, which had been designed to function even during a fire, while some 3,000 tourists were hustled down both elevators and stairs. The blaze, which caused more panic than damage, was out within an hour without casualties. The only recorded problem with a visitor was the one who complained because he was refused the ride to the top during the fire after paying his $3.60.[23]

The Eiffel Tower may not have been sold as many times as the Brooklyn Bridge, but a number of confidence men have nonetheless managed to make money out of it. The story goes that the first was a sharper from Prussian Silesia who claimed in 1891 to have a contract to make a sheath that would protect the tower in winter. He found a businessman in Brandenburg, Germany, willing to put up the funds to purchase miles of canvas—and was never heard from again.[24]

Since then the tower's name has been taken in vain to promote several swindles, often involving recuperation of those 8,000 tons of iron, or painting the tower with special antirust products. One of those recurrent stories in Paris media about the need to tear down the tower prompted such a con in 1925.

Count Victor Lustig, who happened to have at least 23 other known aliases, and his associate, an American known as "Dapper Dan" Collins, were operating in Paris at the time and noticed the article. Lustig contacted five salvage companies, introduced himself as an official from the City of Paris office with jurisdiction over the Eiffel Tower, and invited them to bid for the demolition job. He rented an imposing suite at the Hôtel de Crillon on Place de la Concorde, explaining to the firms' representatives that the ultra-secret negotiations could not be held in his office because of the need for maximum discretion.

Lustig took the highest bid, amounting to several million francs, and then coolly accepted in addition a bribe from his mark before catching the Orient Express for Vienna. The victim was too embarrassed to complain to the police, and Lustig and Collins "sold" the tower a second time before heading for America and a series of highly profitable jobs there. Lustig was finally convicted of counterfeiting in the United States and sent to Alcatraz.[25]

Predictably, terrorists have had the Eiffel Tower in their sights since long before September 11, 2001. Indeed, one of its closest calls came decades ago during France's colonial war with Algeria in the 1950s. Terrorists of the colony's National Liberation Front (NLF) had already exploded bombs in many parts of Paris when they decided to hit the tower in order to knock out the television and radio equipment—including transmitters of the police and gendarmerie important in the fight against crime and terrorism.

On September 23, 1958, shortly after Charles de Gaulle came to power, NLF terrorists planted a five-pound charge of dynamite, attached to a clockwork timer, in the ladies' room on the third platform. The bomb was found the next morning by a cleaning lady, appropriately named Madame Angèle, who alerted the tower's guards and Armand Triffoz, an engineer working for the tower. Triffoz grabbed the bomb and carried it outside so it would cause less damage if it exploded. The police bomb squad arrived and defused the device, which had malfunctioned; they said later that had the bomb gone off as planned, it would have blown away the entire top of the tower. For his heroism, Triffoz was awarded the Silver Medal of the City of Paris, presented by Gustave Eiffel's grandson, René Le Grain-Eiffel.[26]

Four years later, as the colonial war with Algeria was drawing to a close with another French defeat, it was France's extreme rightist Secret Army Organization (SAO) that was throwing the bombs in Paris to protest De Gaulle's policy of independence for Algeria. When the SAO terrorist code-named Castille was arrested, police found complete plans for dynamiting the tower's north pier. With that leg gone, the structure would have collapsed into the Seine.[27]

In December 1994, Muslim fundamentalists already had the idea of using an airliner as a flying bomb, but their target was Paris rather than New York. Four heavily armed members of a militant Algerian Muslim group hijacked an Air France airliner on a runway at Algiers airport and demanded to be flown to Paris. The pilot convinced them that he had to refuel and landed at Marseilles, where the plane sat on the tarmac for 54 hours, during which the terrorists murdered three of the 173 passengers. Finally, a special anti-terrorist unit of the gendarmerie skillfully executed an assault and killed the hijackers, narrowly thwarting their ultimate objective: crashing the plane into the Eiffel Tower.[28]

Post 9/11, security was stepped up at the tower. Security personnel keep it under 24-hour surveillance with 86 closed-circuit television cameras, including 39 with infrared night vision. Gendarmes, often armed with rifles, now patrol beneath it, and for a while, handbags were searched. French authorities know very well that the country's numerous mosques — almost as many now as Christian churches — often serve as terrorist recruitment centers, and its burgeoning Muslim minority of nearly ten percent of the total population makes France an ideal location for sleeper cells: "The threat is real," the Interior Minister has repeated.[29]

Terrorism specialists frequently warn that the Eiffel Tower is a likely target, along with Notre Dame Cathedral, the American embassy, and the presidential home at the Elysée Palace. In fact, a document circulating among Muslim fundamentalists in Belgium explicitly named the tower as a choice target.[30] But except for one bomb alert in October 2001, when the tower was quickly evacuated of its 1,800 tourists following an anonymous telephone call—a thorough search of the structure showed it to be a false alarm—the tower to date has been relatively unaffected by the specter of terrorism.[31]

SEEMINGLY IMPERVIOUS to everything men have tried, from the Belle Epoque to the Age of Anxiety, *la Grande Dame* just keeps on keeping on. Usually some simple rites mark the passage of the years, as when, in 1939, the Duke and Duchess of Windsor presided over a beauty contest to celebrate the tower's 50th anniversary—girls had to be over six feet tall to compete for the title of Miss Eiffel Tower—and Mass was said on the first level.[32]

Tower management presented automobiles to the 25 millionth visitor in 1953 and the 35 millionth in 1959. (The latter was an 11-year-old country lad visiting the capital, who said with charming candor that he would turn the car over to *maman* because all he ever expected to drive was a tractor.)[33] The 1989 centenary was marked by a re-enactment by actors in period costume of the flag-waving inauguration of the tower, as well as Philippe Petits's high-wire act and a fireworks extravaganza.

Meanwhile the Eiffel Tower goes on exercising its quasi-mystical appeal to the masses, who respond to it not only with yearly pilgrimages by the millions, but with a constant flow of fan mail. A random sampling of the dozens of letters received annually by the tower management reveals the range of curiosity and interest the tower sparks in a wide spectrum of humanity.

A Turkish engineer wants to know the exact mathematical formula of the structure's curving columns, for instance, and a high school student in Kansas asks how many tons of paint are required to cover it. The tower received a flowery birthday card on one anniversary from a schoolgirl in Bremen, Germany, and one of her countrymen in the Eifel region wonders who built the Eiffel Tower and, for that matter, "Why do you spell it with two *f*'s?"

The Performing Arts Abroad group in Kalamazoo, Michigan, offers to give a concert on the first platform. A lady restaurateur in California asks the secret of the warmer in the tower's snack bar that heats hot dog buns from the inside. Many ask, with obvious concern, whether it is true that the tower will be torn down. One engineering firm in Bangkok saw a business opportunity in the allegedly tottering tower and offered to rebuild it, noting pointedly that it had already restored Bangkok's Temple of Dawn. And then there is the young lady in Vermont who asks, "Why do all the people come to the tower? What has the tower got inside?"[34]

In a way, her questions are the same as those that many have attempted to answer over the years. For, implicit in the foolishness and drama that have attended it during its history, is the unexpected significance that man's tallest pure tower has assumed. Created to proclaim France's prancing pride, the tower has become an object of fascination and obsession, a touchstone and totem of surprising evocative power, as 20th-century artists, poets, and philosophers were to discover.

Universal Symbol

WHEN GUSTAVE EIFFEL died in 1923, his tower was still the tallest manmade edifice of any sort in the world. It would remain so until 1929—a reign of exactly 40 years—when the 1,046-foot Chrysler Building was completed in New York, followed by the 1,250-foot Empire State Building two years later.

Since then, utilitarian structures over a thousand feet tall have become commonplace. Modern techniques permit prosaic factory chimneys to reach over a quarter of a mile high. In the last few decades television masts have proliferated across the globe from one in Tokyo frankly modeled on the Eiffel Tower and standing 1,092 feet tall, to a 1,750-footer of reinforced concrete in Moscow, a guyed antenna near Fargo, North Dakota, 2,063 feet tall, equivalent to the Eiffel Tower, Washington Monument, and Great Pyramid together.[1]

Towers are rivaled in height by high-rise apartment and office buildings. Architects today consider 3,000-foot skyscrapers feasible. Even Paris, where the Eiffel Tower provoked such heated protests just over a century ago, is now ringed about with unimaginative tall buildings possessing all the aesthetic appeal of shoeboxes stood on end and none of the tower's doughty originality. Parisians complain halfheartedly about them—particularly the hideous, 690-foot Tour Maine-Montparnasse, the tallest building in Europe, which dominates the city like some dark Moloch—but the days are long past when they cared enough about the beauty of their city to risk appearing quixotic in combating such eyesores.

And yet despite the frenzied construction of television antennas and multistory buildings, the Eiffel Tower is in some sense still the tallest. Every taller structure since has had some specific commercial or useful purpose, either as a communications tool or shelter. Not since the Exposition of 1889 has anyone thrown up so high a tower *qua* tower, a ladder to the sky with no other fundamental purpose than allowing man to climb up and have a look around. Never again was the persistent human impulse so great to express a people's aspiration and accomplishment through erection of a gratuitously tall structure.

The British, to be sure, wanted to better the French as soon as the Eiffel Tower was up. Hardly had the Paris Exposition closed than Benjamin Baker, celebrated builder of the Forth Bridge, opened a contest for designs of a 1,200-foot tower. Seventy projects were submitted and two were awarded prizes, although the jury admitted that "The existence of the Eiffel Tower and the desire to avoid imitating it considerably increase the difficulty of the problem, for it represents the most rational use of architectural and economic means." Sincere flattery indeed, coming from the British.[2]

Work on Britain's iron tower began in June 1893 in Wembley Park, near London. Seven months later the structure had reached the level of the Eiffel Tower's first platform, but the project gave out at that point. London had to wait nearly a century for its tall tower, the ungainly and thoroughly utilitarian Post Office Tower, at 620 feet not quite two-thirds as tall as Eiffel's creation.

The impulse continues to exercise men's imaginations, but designers keep bumping up against the problem confronting Benjamin Baker: the Eiffel Tower is inimitable.

For the World's Fair of 1932, Chicago wanted to build a 2,060-foot steel tower that would accommodate 4,000 people on its observation platform, but the $3 million project never came off. Saint Louis' steel Gateway Arch, completed in 1965 at a cost of $29 million, gets around the difficulty of imitating the Eiffel Tower by being a parabolic curve, but it rises "only" 630 feet.[3]

In Paris itself an artist named Nicholas Schoffer advanced a harebrained scheme in 1972 for a "cybernetic light tower" 1,300 feet tall to be constructed among the high-rise office buildings in the suburb of La Défense. A rectangular metal cage, the tower was to be equipped with multicolored, electronically programmed flashing

The Eiffel Tower compared to the tallest structures in the world at the time of its construction. (Photo RMN)

lights and revolving mirrors to create random patterns in the Paris sky. It was also to cost $40 million, a figure that, if nothing else did it, apparently deterred Paris authorities from authorizing what surely would have been the city's ultimate visual nightmare.

Other present-day builders of towers simply pattern their designs on the Eiffel Tower—or dream of importing it whole. A 340-foot replica of the tower was built in King's Mill, Ohio, as part of a theme park in 1972. Miami entertained the idea of constructing a thousand-foot tower for its Inter-American Center in conjunction with the United States Bicentennial in 1976; executives of the construction firm studying the project visited the Eiffel Tower in September 1972 and talked with Eiffel Tower Company engineers about how Eiffel did it.[4]

Montreal wanted a tall tower for its Expo 67 and first considered transporting the Eiffel Tower to the Ile Sainte Hélène. When this was shown to be impracticable, the fair's organizers had plans drawn up for a structure taller than Eiffel's and invited the City of Paris to help finance it. Paris declined, and Montreal abandoned the idea.

Another attempt to import the tower was made by a real estate man in North Myrtle Beach, South Carolina, in 1974, after he was told by a waggish guide during a visit to Paris that the Eiffel Tower was for sale. He decided that it was just the thing his town needed. With support from city officials he applied to the Federal Aviation Agency for permission to put a thousand-foot tower in the area of the local airport. After all, he explained to a reporter, "They took the London Bridge and moved it over here brick by brick." But as it happened, the tower was not for sale.[5]

Latest version of the Eiffel Tower was created by that theme park for adults, Las Vegas. When a new 34-story, 2,916-room casino resort opened in 1999, it had its own 50-story, half-scale copy of the tower, with three of its four legs rising from the casino floor and going through the roof. Complete with restaurant 100 feet up and an observation deck overlooking the neon charms of Las Vegas Boulevard, America's latest version of the tower means, as one newspaper cheerfully put it, "Now you can always have Paris—sort of—even if you never get to France."[6]

IMAGES OF THE TOWER in every conceivable form have been popular since the Exposition of 1889. Indeed, the question of souvenirs got Gustave Eiffel into a lawsuit early in the tower's first year of existence, for he had granted exclusive rights to the Printemps department store to make and sell tower trinkets. He had reckoned without the power of France's artisans and small shopkeepers, who won a class-action suit against him for the right to part of the business.

Since then the variety of objects for sale bearing the tower's likeness has multiplied beyond the fondest dreams of French *schlockmeisters.* The items number at least several hundred, including the numerous versions of miniature towers from the size of a bracelet charm to table lamps and on and on. Then there are the everyday objects struck with the tower in some form, including cuff links, ladies' compacts, atomizers, table flatware, penknives, scissors, paperweights, letter openers, cane heads, umbrella handles, cigar cutters, cigarette holders, pipes, scarves, brooches, wine glasses — the inventory seems endless. It is said that the only visitor to the tower who ever bought one of every item on sale was Japan's Emperor Hirohito. Surveys of Paris department stores reveal that the tower comes first in the hearts of American souvenir hunters, but that the history-minded British prefer busts of Napoleon.

The pervasive desire for a replica or relic — and I freely admit having one of its heavy, cast-off rivets on my desk — of the Eiffel Tower goes beyond mere souvenirs and takes on the dimension of fetishism. The number of model Eiffel Towers lovingly made by individuals under its benign charm is unknown, but several have come to light over the years, cases amazing for the hours spent in painstaking thoroughness.

In the 1930s, a dental student in New York built a ceiling-high scale model Eiffel Tower, appropriately enough of 11,000 toothpicks. In 1963, a five-foot model was made in Buenos Aires, also of toothpicks, but with a difference — they came from 57 countries. In France, a watchmaker named Georges Vitel mobilized his wife and son every weekend and holiday for several years to put together a model incorporating 2.5 million matchsticks and 2,000 feet of electrical wiring. Eight thousand hours of work by the trio produced a one-tenth scale model of fanatical detail down to working elevators, electric lights, tables and chairs in the tower's restaurants, and a bed in Gustave Eiffel's third platform apartment.[7]

American cultists include an Ohioan who in 1972 wrote the Eiffel Tower Company for the tower's exact dimensions, then built a seven-foot model of 704 hand-cut pieces of perforated aluminum. About the same time, Howard Porter of Detroit wrote for data and then spent 300 hours on a $1/_{250}$ scale model using 110 fireplace matches, 1,080 ordinary kitchen matches, and 1,200 toothpicks, which he assembled with half a pound of glue and a pair of locking dental tweezers. Porter kept tower management informed of his progress with letters and photographs, and climaxed his labors in 1974 with a trip to Paris, where I met him, for his first view of the real tower and lunch on the second platform with tower officials.[8]

WITH PASSING TIME, the Eiffel Tower appears to assume an increasing status as talisman of the modern world. It was invoked, for instance, at the New York World's Fair of 1964-1965 as a sort of patron saint of progress in building and design.

When construction of the fair's symbol, the stainless steel Unisphere, began with a ceremony in Flushing Meadow on March 6, 1963, René Le Grain-Eiffel and Baron Alexis de Gunzburg, then president of the Eiffel Tower Company, were invited to attend. One hundred forty feet tall and weighing 40,000 pounds, Unisphere was seen by the fair's organizers and its makers, the U. S. Steel Corporation, as a continuation of the Eiffel Tower idea. As the president of U. S. Steel, Roger Blough, explained at the ceremony:

> This tower was the product of the genius and the daring of one
> of the great builders, Alexandre Gustave Eiffel, who also pioneered
> the use of the materials of his day in structurally designed concepts

for bridges, buildings and viaducts, even before his imagination and courage produced the great tower of which we speak. It is most appropriate that as we begin the construction of Unisphere, we pause in tribute to a man whose technical achievements have inspired so much progress in building and in design.[9]

Mr. Blough then presented to Gustave Eiffel's grandson a stainless steel plaque engraved with juxtaposed drawings of the Eiffel Tower and Unisphere, and the text:

> Man's achievement in an expanding universe. Eiffel Tower, 1889, Unisphere, 1964. Commemorating start of construction of Unisphere. The theme symbol of the New York World's Fair, 1964-1965, and honoring Gustave Eiffel, magician in iron, engineer, designer, master builder, innovator and creator of Eiffel Tower, symbol of the 1889 Paris International Exposition.

Later, when the 100-story John Hancock Center in Chicago was topped out on May 6, 1968, the insurance firm placed a memento of the Eiffel Tower atop the 1,107-foot skyscraper's steel framework. At a ceremony held exactly 79 years after the opening of the tower, the company affixed a time capsule, whimsically called a Skystone, to the roof of the building, which was then the second tallest in the world after the Empire State. Into the capsule went an original letter signed by John Hancock, a fragment of wood from the Hancock House in Boston, historical books and documents — and, like including a bit of the True Cross in a reliquary, a triangular wedge of iron from the Eiffel Tower flown over aboard an Air France airliner.[10]

Even Paris has officially reconciled itself to the tower, albeit long after the structure had been wholeheartedly accepted by Parisians and become the city's de facto totem. On the occasion of Gustave Eiffel's death, the tower was eulogized nearly as much as its creator; one mass circulation newspaper stated that, "All in all, this audacious construction is a veritable chef d'oeuvre of French art."

Masterpiece or not, the tower became even more ubiquitous and unavoidable than Maupassant could have imagined in his worst fits of depression over it. Since the early days of the century, no map or other schema of Paris, scarcely a travel poster or advertisement associated with France has appeared without an image of the tower to create immediate identification.

When managers of one of France's largest-circulation newspapers, *France-Soir*, wanted to state visually the equivalent of the old ad, "In Philadelphia, nearly everybody reads the *Bulletin*," they put up posters showing an Eiffel Tower in a sitting position reading their paper. And when a big French bank, Crédit Lyonnais, wanted to advertise the opening of a branch in New York, its full-page ads in American magazines showed not a bank, but an Eiffel Tower superimposed over the buildings of lower Manhattan.

Not until 1964 did the French government finally recognize the tower as an important part of the country's heritage. André Malraux as Minister of Culture declared the structure a historical monument, insuring that it may not be altered in any way without special authorization. Roland Barthes, the noted French philosopher, observes that, "The surprising thing is that Paris waited so long to acquire its symbol. The Eiffel Tower became Paris through metonymy."[11]

Another French thinker, Philippe Barrès, holds that the tower is as important a part of Paris' mystique as any other monument in this city of symbols:

> Notre Dame represents the Faith, the Institute and University are the life of the mind, the Panthéon is service rendered to the nation, the Elysée Palace symbolizes the State, the Louvre art and history, the Arch of Triumph and the Invalides mean glory. Even the Eiffel Tower, so often criticized, has its meaning for us. At the turn of the century it symbolized the vitality of our know-how which keeps us at the forefront of modern competition.[12]

The Eiffel Tower did not have to wait for official recognition to become a subject for poets, painters, and pundits. Hardly had the mini-tempest of the artists' protest died down when Paris songwriters began turning out ditties about the tower for the edification of crowds along the Belle Epoque's teeming boulevards. One popular song of the period called "At 300 Meters Up" begins, "What vertigo it gives you! / Paris so grandiose doesn't look like much / At 300 meters up," and goes on to recount the adventures of pretty, complaisant ladies under the tower's spell on the third platform, the peccadillos of stereotyped English tourists, and the like.

Another song saw everyone profiting from the tower, including cafe owners, taxi drivers and so on, but with cobblers making the biggest windfall profits of all, "Because the tower is 900 feet." Still another described an Eiffel Tower raising its head high in the sky, mocking Garnier, Dumas and Meissonier, and gaily challenging passing clouds, "Halt or I'll cut you in two!" Probably the best-known of all, popularized by Maurice Chevalier and Patachou to the point of becoming the Eiffel Tower's theme song, goes:

> *Paris, mais c'est la tour Eiffel*
> *Avec sa pointe qui monte au ciel*
> *Qu'on la trouve laide, qu'on la trouve belle*
> *Y'a pas d'Paris sans tour Eiffel.*
> *On la débine, on la charrie,*
> *Pourtant, partout ce n'est qu'un cri ·*
> *Paris n's'rait pas Paris sans elle,*
> *Paris, mais c'est la tour Eiffel!*

During the First World War a poem praised the tower's role as communications center for the French Army: "We know that by night you give the orders for the battle, / That by day you guide it. And we think you are beautiful / Both fortress and lace." And during the dismal days of Nazi occupation, the cabaret star Mistinguette heartened Parisians nightly by singing "The Eiffel Tower Is Still There" in her review at the Casino de Paris.

The tower began to win its place in literature in the 1920s, with poet Jean Cocteau's ballet-play, *Les Mariés de la Tour Eiffel*, in which it served as backdrop for a gentle satire of La Belle Epoque. But Cocteau, an icon of Paris' artistic/literary scene, treated the tower gallantly as "Notre Dame of the Left Bank . . . the queen of Paris." In a later work he called the tower affectionately "a cage of bluebirds."[13]

Suddenly the tower became a legitimate subject for French poets. Guillaume Apollinaire, friend of Pablo Picasso and herald of Surrealism, called it "The shepherdess of the clouds." Expanding his metaphor, he began one poem, "Shepherdess, O Eiffel Tower, your flock of bridges is bleating this morning." During the war, Apollinaire thumbed his nose at the Nazis with a saucy poem innocuously entitled "The Eiffel Tower," which by graphic legerdemain managed to insult the occupiers without their knowing it. The letters of the poem were composed to form the outline of the tower, making them difficult to read by anyone whose French was shaky. But the message easily got through to Apollinaire's French public: "Hello world, of which I am the eloquent tongue which your mouth, O Paris, will forever stick out at the Germans."[14]

"The staircase to infinity" was what the Symbolist-Surrealist poet Léon-Paul Fargue grandly termed the tower on one occasion. On another, he called it "The *i* of Paris firing its dot like a glorious cannon towards the beauty of interstellar space." And the poet admitted to peculiar visions: "I can hear the Eiffel Tower falling down. Its dinosaur's tail ends at Brest or Toulon. And along with my 40 million countrymen, I am buried in broken lamps and shreds of sky. In the morning the proud giraffe has grown a hundred meters taller."[15]

The novelist and playwright Jean Giraudoux was probably the writer most impressed by the tower, judging by his published reactions to it. He first of all found it an excellent vantage point from which to admire his favorite city, "the thousand acres of the world where most has been thought, spoken and written. The planet's hub, the most free, the most elegant, the least hypocritical." He also playfully expressed his admiration of Eiffel's achievement in "My Pretty Eiffel Tower":

> *Mon Dieu*, what confidence its engineer possessed in universal gravity. Holy Virgin, if the law of gravity had been contradicted for only a quarter of a second, what a magnificent catastrophe it would have been! But this is what can be created with hypotheses. Here, realized in iron, is the rope thrown to the sky by the fakir, and which he invites his friends to climb. *Mon Dieu*, how beautiful it is. . . ."[16]

But poets were tardy in discovering the Eiffel Tower, compared with painters, who immediately saw its visual potency and savored, as one aesthete put it, Eiffel's "purely dynamic conception of space." As early as 1889, Georges Seurat did a magnificent pointillist canvas full of shimmering, parti-colored light, as though the tower were seen through a luminous mist. At the same time, an impressionist, Louis Hayet, a protégé of Pissarro's, saw the tower in the Paris cityscape as the natural counterpoint to the obelisk in Place de la Concorde — still one of the best places from which to view the tower.

Aesthetically, the Eiffel Tower had much in common with modern art, being, like modern paintings and sculptures, an end in itself, its own subject. That may partly explain why it figured in works by many of the great artists whose names are synonymous with 20th-century art: Pablo Picasso, Marc Chagall, Camille Pissarro, Marcel Gromaire, Raoul Dufy, Henri Rousseau, Maurice Utrillo, and Kees van Dongen, among others, representing the Impressionist, Fauve, Cubist and Futurist schools and their offshoots. For them the tower seems to have been the inevitable subject, one whose mathematical definition of space drew them like a magnet.

Of them all, the most fascinated was Robert Delaunay, whose Cubistic vision dissected the structure from every possible point of view in an important series of paintings done from 1909 to 1911. Influenced initially by Cezanne and Seurat, Delaunay was on his way to becoming one of the precursors of nonfigurative painting, breaking down a subject into prisms of color; his work had impact on the German Blue Riders such as Paul Klee, and eventually inspired a related style among American painters like S. Macdonald-Wright and Morgan Russell, which was the first move in the United States toward abstract art. The French poet Blaise Cendrars was a close friend of Delaunay's during those years and described the artist's dilemma in portraying the tower:

> In 1911, Delaunay did, I believe, 51 canvases of the Eiffel Tower before getting the desired result. No artistic formula known could resolve plastically the case of the tower. Realism diminished the

impression of height; the old laws of Italian perspective made it look skinny. When we viewed it from a distance, it dominated Paris, stiff and perpendicular; when we approached it, it seemed to bend and lean over us. Seen from the first platform it twisted, and seen from the top it appeared to fold in upon itself, legs spread and neck pulled in. Delaunay wanted not only to show the tower, but also to situate it in Paris.

Finally he took the tower apart in order to place it in its natural framework. He truncated it and inclined it to give the impression of vertigo it inspires; he adopted 10 different viewpoints, 15 perspectives so that part of it is seen from below, part from above, while the buildings around it are shown from left and right, from above and below. . . .[17]

The tower has also inspired film makers. Many films have been shot using it as setting or theme, perhaps the most memorable being *The Lavender Hill Mob*, in which Alec Guiness is involved in a plot to transport gold stolen from the Bank of England in the form of miniature Eiffel Towers, and which ends in a chase scene through the tower's girders.

In France, René Clair has been the *cineaste* most fascinated by the tower. He began his film-making career in 1924 with a work of science fiction, *Paris Qui Dort*, in which a mad scientist anesthetized the population of Paris except for a handful of persons who happened to be on the tower's third platform. Then Clair, who liked to say "The Eiffel Tower is my village," returned to the tower in 1928 to do a lyrical documentary devoted entirely to it, and called simply *La Tour*. He treated the tower as an abstraction, using a few special effects such as making the elevators approach each other on the same track and then fuse and disappear, but mainly concentrating on impressions of webbing and tracery produced by girders and trusswork. The result is a masterful study of the Eiffel Tower as archetype, conveying a compelling feeling of mechanical intricacy and vertiginous height.

The tower deconstructed by Robert Delaunay in 1910.

EXAMINING THE TOWER rather later than artists and poets, some intellectuals have discovered in it a rich mine of metaphor and meaning. Its historical significance has been pointed out by several, though seldom in the sweeping terms of one French sociologist, Joseph Foliet, who sees the tower as the most apt label for our era. "European civilization," he declares, "after having been Roman, Carolingian, Gothic, Renaissance, and Baroque, has become in the 20th century the civilization of the Eiffel Tower."[18]

Roland Barthes, whose writings on the symbols and signs of semiotics made him the highly influential leader of the Structuralist and New Criticism movements in Europe and the United States, has probably done more high-flown philosophizing about the tower than any other thinker, having devoted an entire book to it. He finds that the tower and Notre Dame Cathedral form Paris' symbolic couple: past and present, stone and metal, sacred and profane.

For Barthes, the stone-metal dichotomy is especially important in understanding the new departure the tower stood for. "The history of iron is one of the most progressivist there is," he writes. "Eiffel crowned that history by making iron the sole material of his constructions and by imagining an object entirely of iron (the tower) raised in the sky of Paris like a stele consecrated to Iron: in this material is synthesized all the Balzacian and Faustian passion of the century." Conceptually, Barthes finds that the tower eludes reason, which demands purpose, by being "fully useless."

Being non-utilitarian, far from being a fault, frees it from mundane, earthbound considerations to play higher role as

> a great baroque dream which touches the limits of the irrational. . . . In fact, the tower is *nothing*, it achieves a sort of absolute zero as a monument. It is part of no ceremony, not even that of Art. It cannot be visited like a museum, for there is nothing to see *in* the tower. And yet this empty monument receives each year twice as many visitors as the Louvre and many times more than the largest cinema in Paris. Why then does one visit the tower? Doubtless to participate in a dream of which it is more the crystallizer than the object, transforming the touristic rite into an

adventure of observation and intelligence. . . . Every visitor to the tower becomes a philosophical structuralist without knowing it, spontaneously distinguishing discrete points of Paris and linking and ordering them in his mind: nothing could be less passive than the view of Paris from the tower.

The tower is the ultimate, universal symbol:

> Beyond its role as symbol of Paris, it touches the human imagination in the most general way. Its simple, matrixial form confers on it the vocation of infinite integer: one after the other, depending on our imagination, it becomes the symbol of Paris, of modernity, of communication, of science or the 19th century, a rocket, stem, derrick, phallus, lightning rod or insect. In the great domain of dreams, it is the inevitable sign. . . . It is impossible to flee this pure sign, *for it means everything*.

The tower's all-embracing symbolism explains the number of suicides on it, he believes, for "despite or because of the innumerable images of life that it gives rise to, it calls down the last image of human experience, that of death."[19]

Barthes is nearly rivaled in the manipulation of heavy theses by Maurice Besset, another French intellectual who has reflected on the Eiffel Tower at length. He sees it as "A monument to itself, created by the century of the mechanistic revolution, the century that overturned all social and aesthetic principles."

In particular, Besset describes the tower's builder as "the creator of Eiffelian space," ordering and resolving the rhythms and tensions of forces on the tower with a muscular feeling for space that renders it "an indivisible, living reality, a fluid into which he insinuates himself and against which — the wind — he struggles." Thanks to Eiffel's mastery of "interior and exterior space," the tower becomes for those who behold it "a new form and a new dimension of structured space," inviting the spectator to experience new spatiotemporal relationships.

And Besset underlines the coincidence of Eiffel's design of the tower with the era of Impressionist painting, both tending toward a dynamic conception of space: the Impressionists by breaking down their subjects into pure light, Eiffel by rejecting static masonry for more flexible iron. "It is therefore as a function of an entire aesthetic culture . . . that we see and interpret his tower today."[20]

Inevitably in the land of soaring cathedrals, French thinkers have compared the tower to the work of Gothic builders. "The profound relationship of this art of bolted iron with that of Gothic art" was pointed out by a French historian, François Poncetton, who explained:

> The Gothic architects also strived for height. They also supported their vaults with columns, using an absolute minimum of materials. And [like the tower's arches] the walls of their churches are illusory, being no more than filling between the piers. Stand before the great rose windows or the most window-riddled sections of walls and observe and feel the force lines crossing through the vaults: you will find in these daring leaps a foreshadowing of the aerial art of Eiffel.[21]

But of those who have written and thought deeply about the tower, the man who is perhaps best qualified has expressed his views most simply. The architect Le Corbusier, who found all of Eiffel's designs marked by "an admirable instinct for proportion," had a personal affection for the tower. At the time of the Arts Décoratifs Exposition in Paris in 1925, he wrote that "The Eiffel Tower has entered the domain of architecture. In 1889 it was the aggressive expression of calculations. In 1900 the aesthetes wanted to demolish it. In 1925 it dominates the Arts Déco Exposition. Rising above the plaster palaces with their twisted décor, it looks pure as a crystal."[22]

Later, having himself become an architectural legend as leader of the functional International school of building, Le Corbusier wrote, "I bear witness to the tower as an indefatigable pilgrim who has crisscrossed the world. In the cities, in the savanna, in the pampa, in the desert, on the gats and on the estuaries, everywhere, and among the humble as among the others, the tower is in everyone's heart as the sign of a beloved Paris. Such homage is due to the qualities of a man, of a place, and of an epoch."[23]

Epilogue

Cenotaph of the Belle Epoque, cynosure of the postindustrial era, the Eiffel Tower stands today as a watershed emblem. In its time it was briefly the highest high-tech program of the day, carrying technical innovation to a logical absurdity in order to reassure a nation in need of it.

Now it seems to me to represent a culmination of the human race's naïve enthusiasm for machines. It was a blissful period ignorant that machines would shortly be used to devastating effect across the fields of Flanders in one of Europe's worst wars. The tower's innocent exuberance underscores the brevity of our stay in the Industrial Eden, when we could still believe wholeheartedly in the unlimited benefits of technology.

The chances are that man's historically tallest tower will continue to acquire overlays of significance in an age increasingly short of meaning. Its role as talisman reminds me of a perceptive remark that Claude Lévi-Strauss, the great French anthropologist, once made to me during a long interview about the state of religion today. "What secular modern man worships more than anything else," he said, "is his own development and the objects that have marked its high points over the ages." Thus the relatively recent veneration of everything antique, from Greek ruins to pre-Columbian art objects, to Renaissance paintings, Russian icons, and even old locomotives and automobiles. Similarly, the Eiffel Tower appears destined for an ever-greater place in our collective nostalgia.

For the present, it enough that it continue to crane over the Seine, looking old-fashioned and gawky, revealing itself at a glance rather than affronting the world with smug rectangularity. To me, it looks vulnerable in its honesty, and I feel a certain affection for it despite its kitschy role as plaything of the masses. The Eiffel Tower reminds me who we were and, by inference, who we are.

Acknowledgments

MY RESEARCH for this book was greatly facilitated by the generous assistance of Monsieur René Le Grain-Eiffel. Born the year of his grandfather's tower was completed, he made available to me in Paris the unpublished memoirs of Gustave Eiffel and a number of other documents difficult of access. For this I am grateful.

Valued help was also extended by other members of the Eiffel family. Henriette Venot, a granddaughter of Eiffel, and her husband, Louis, kindly opened to me their private collection of Eiffeliana in the village of Salleboeuf, near Bordeaux. Madame André Granet, another granddaughter, lent me certain documents from her personal library in Paris.

The Bureau International des Expositions in Paris helpfully put at my disposal its unique library of works on the world's great fairs. The Société Nouvelle d'Exploitation de la Tour Eiffel also made documentation available, as did the Beaugrenelle municipal library in Paris.

I also wish to express the customary author's thanks to my wife, Claudie, and son, Christopher, for their support, and for accepting with forbearance my necessary absences from family life when writing this.

J. H.

Statistics

Number of iron structural components in tower	15,000
Number of rivets	2,500,000
Weight of foundations	277,602 kilograms (306 tons)
Weight of iron	7,341,214 kilograms (8,092.2 tons)
Weight of elevator systems	946,000 kilograms (1,042.8 tons)
Total weight	8,564,816 kilograms (9,441 tons)
Pressure on foundations	4.1 to 4.5 kilograms per square centimeter, depending on pier (58.26 to 64 lbs per square inch)
Height of first platform	57.63 meters (189 feet)
Height of second platform	115.73 meters (379 feet 8 inches)
Height of third platform	276.13 meters (905 feet 11 inches)
Total height in 1889	300.51 meters (985 feet 11 inches)
Total height with television antenna	318 meters (1,043 feet 4 inches)
Number of antennas now attached to top	116
Number of steps to top	1,671
Maximum sway at top caused by wind	12 centimeters (4¾ inches)
Maximum sway at top caused by dilation	18 centimeters (7 inches)
Weight of paint/frequency	60 tons every seven years
Lighting today	336 sodium lamps
Size of base area	10,281.96 square meters (2.54 acres)
Dates of construction	26 January 1887 to 31 March 1889
Cost of construction	7,799,401.31 francs ($1,505,675.90)
Number of visitors at Exposition of 1889	1,968,287
Total receipts at Exposition of 1889	5,919,884 francs ($1,142,834.70)

Principal Engineering Projects
of *G. Eiffel et Compagnie*

1865: Train stations at Toulouse and Agen, France

1866: Fine Arts and Archeology pavilions for Paris Exposition of 1867

1867 to 1869: Bridges for railway line from Poitiers to Limoges, France; viaducts at Neuvial and over Sioule River for Orléans Railway, France; Church of Notre Dame des Champs, Paris; Jewish temple, Paris; gasworks, Versailles

1870: Bridges for railway lines from Latour to Millau, and Brive to Tulle, France; swing bridge at Dieppe, France

1872: Bridges for railway line from Jassy to Ungheni, Romania; harbor installations and customs house for port of Arica, Chile; bridges at La Oroya, Peru

1873: Gasworks at La Paz, Bolivia

1874: Locks for dam on Moskva River, Russia

1875: Church at Tacna, Peru; church at Manila, Philippines; casino at Sables d'Olonne, France

1876: Bridges for Vendée Railway, France; bridges for Gerona line, Spain; Maria Pia Bridge at Oporto, Portugal

1877: Viana Bridge, Portugal; train station at Pest, Hungary; monumental entrance and City of Paris pavilion for Paris Exposition of 1878

1878: Bridges for Chemin de Fer du Midi, France; bridges for Cáceres line, Spain; gasworks at Clichy, France

1879: Bridges for railway from Ploesti to Predeal, Romania; bridge at Oued Djemma, Algeria; structural work for enlargement of Bon Marché department store, Paris; annex to Magasins du Louvre department store, Paris

1880: Bridges on Beira Alta line, Portugal; bridge over Tagus River, Spain; bridges at Binh Dien, Tan An, and Ben Luc, Cochin China; bridge at Sidi Moussa, Algeria; bridge over Dordogne River at Saint André de Cubzac, France

1881: Bridge over Danube River at Szeged, Hungary; headquarters of Crédit Lyonnais bank, Paris; train stations at San Sebastián and Santander, Spain; dam on Seine River at Port Mort, France; interior structure of Statue of Liberty, Paris

1882: Bridge over Dordogne River at Bergerac, France; bridges on Asturias line, Spain; bridge at Saigon, Cochin China; covered market at Bordeaux, France

1883: Bridges over the Tardes River and at Charenton and Sainte Claire d'Oloron, France; gasworks at Rennes, France

1884: Bridge at Cholon, Cochin China; viaduct at Garabit, France; steel mill at Pagny-sur-Meuse, France; structural work of Galliéra Museum, Paris

1885: Bridges and train stations for line from Lisbon to Cintra, Portugal; rotating dome for Nice Observatory, France

1889: Thousand-foot tower for Paris Exposition of 1889; locks for Panama Canal

Bibliography

"An Account of the Exercises on the Occasion of the Presentation of the Langley medal and the Unveiling of the Langley Memorial Tablet, May 6, 1913, including the Addresses." Washington: The Smithsonian Institution, 1913.

"Les Artistes Contre la Tour Eiffel." Résumé de Conversation avec Monsieur Eiffel." *Le Temps*, 14 February 1887.

Barral, Georges and Jacques. *Histoire Populaire des 72 Savants de la Tour Eiffel*. Paris: J. Mersch, 1889.

Barthes, Roland. *La Tour Eiffel*. Paris: Delpire Editeur, 1964.

Barry, Joseph. "Eiffel, Versatile Engineer-Builder of Towering Talents." *Smithsonian*, April 1972, pp. 49-53.

Besset, Maurice. *Eiffel*. Paris: Hatier, 1957.

Billings, Henry. *Bridges*. New York: The Viking Press, 1956.

Blough, Roger M. Remarks on occasion of dedication of Unisphere and first ground-breaking at New York World's Fair site, 6 March 1963.

Blume, Mary. "The Showman from Paris." *International Herald Tribune*, 22 December 1973.

Bouvier, J. *Les Deux Scandales de Panama*. Paris: Julliard, 1964.

Braibant, Charles. *Histoire de la Tour Eiffel*. Paris: Librairie Plon, 1964.

Bryan, J. "The Eiffel Tower." *Holiday*, May 1955, pp. 19 et seq.

"Bulletin de la Société de Géographie, juin 1879." Paris: Librairie Ch. Delagrave, 1879.

"Cashing In on Its 75 Years." *Business Week*, 16 May 1964, p. 31.

Cobban, Alfred. *A History of Modern France*. 3 vols. Harmondsworth: Penguin Books Ltd., 1965.

Collins, Larry, and Lapierre, Dominique. *Is Paris Burning?* New York: Simon and Schuster, 1965.

Condit, Carl W. *American Building*. Chicago: University of Chicago Press, 1968.

_____. *The Rise of the Skyscraper*. Chicago: University of Chicago Press, 1952.

Cook, Don. "Landmark on the Seine." *Saturday Evening Post*, 11 August 1962, pp. 26-29.

Cordat, Charles. *La Tour Eiffel*. Paris: Les Editions de Minuit, 1955.

Dansette, A. *Les Affaires de Panama*. Paris: Perrin, 1934.

D'Aragon, Marie. *Paris, Tour Eiffel*. Paris: Grange Batelière, 1973.

De Nansouty, Max. *Projet d'une Tour Colossal en Fer de 300 Mètres de Hauteur*. Paris: Le Génie Civil, 1884.

De Vries, Leonard. *Victorian Inventions*. New York: American Heritage Press, 1971.

Eiffel, Gustave. *Notice sur le Pont du Douro à Porto*. Paris: Paul Dupont, 1879.

_____. *Notice sur les différents types de pont portatifs, system Eiffel*. Paris, 1885.

_____. *Notice sur le Viaduc de Garabit près Saint Flour*. Paris: Paul Dupont, 1888.

_____. *Les Grandes Constructions Métalliques*. Paris: Imprimerie Chaix, 1888.

_____. "Conference sur la Tour de trois cents mètres faite à la Société Centrale du Travail Professionel à l'École des Hautes Études Commerciales, 20 novembre 1889." Paris, 1889.

_____. *La Tour de Trois Cents Mètres*. Paris: Imprimerie Mercier, 1900.

_____. *Travaux Scientifiques Exécutés à la Tour de Trois Cents Mètres*. Paris: Maretheux, 1900.

_____. *La Tour Eiffel en 1900*. Paris: Masson et Cie, 1902.

_____. *Dix Années d'Observations Météorologiques à Sèvres (S. & O.) de 1892 à 1901*. Paris: Maretheux, 1907.

_____. *Recherches Experimentales sur la Résistance de l'Air Exécutées à la Tour Eiffel*. Paris: Maretheux, 1907.

_____. *Inauguration du Nouveau Laboratoire Aérodynamique*. Paris: Maretheux, 1912.

_____. *The Resistance of the Air and Aviation*. Boston: Houghton Mifflin Co., 1913.

_____. *Études sur l'Hélice Aérienne, faites au Laboratoire d'Auteuil*. Paris: E. Chiron, Librairie Aéronautique, 1920.

_____. "Généalogie de la Famille Eiffel; Biographie Industrielle et Scientifique," 4 vols., unpublished, completed in 1923.

"Eiffel Tower for Myrtle Beach?" *Atlanta Constitution*, 22 January 1974.

The Eiffel Tower Report of the Smithsonian Institution. Washington, D. C., 1889.

L'Exposition de Paris 1889. Paris: La Librairie Illustrée, 1889.

Exposition Universelle Internationale de 1889 à Paris. Catalogue Général Officiel. Lille: Imprimerie L. Danel, 1889.

Ferrié, Guillet, Lemarchand and Martin. *Discours Prononcés à l'Inauguration du Monument de G. Eiffel, 2 mai 1929*. Paris, 1929.

Fitch, James Marston. *American Building: The Historical Forces That Shaped It*. Vol. 1. Boston: Houghton Mifflin Co., 1966.

Furnas, C. C. and McCarthy, Joe. *The Engineer*. New York: Time, Inc., 1966.

Genêt. "Letter from Paris: Seventy-fifth Anniversary of Eiffel Tower." *The New Yorker*, 16 May 1964, pp.176-177.

Giniger, Henry. "Monsieur Eiffel's Fancy." *The New York Times Magazine*, 7 June 1953.

"Gold Mine in the Sky." *Newsweek*, 18 June 1962, pp. 69-70.

"I Grandi Viodotti di Eiffel nel Massif Central." *Zodiac 13: International Magazine of Contemporary Architecture.* Milan: Edizioni di Comunità, n.d.

Guy, Christian. *Une Tour Nommée Eiffel.* Paris: Presses de la Cité, 1957.

Handlin, Oscar. *Statue of Liberty.* New York: Newsweek Book Division, 1971.

Hawkins, Eric. *Hawkins of the Paris Herald.* New York: Simon and Schuster, 1963.

Henderson, W. O. *The Industrialization of Europe 1780-1914.* London: Thames & Hudson, 1969.

Hobsbawm, E. J. *The Age of Revolution.* London: Weidenfeld and Nicolson, 1962.

Igot, Yves. *Gustave Eiffel.* Paris: Didier, 1962.

Inauguration du Nouveau Laboratoire Aéro-dynamique de M. G. Eiffel, 19 mars 1912. Paris: Maretheux, 1912.

Johnson, James F. and Miller, Floyd. *The Man Who Sold the Eiffel Tower.* New York: Doubleday and Co., 1961.

Josephy, Alvin M., Jr., ed. *The American Heritage History of Flight.* New York: American Heritage Publishing Co., 1962.

"Jumping-Off Place." *Time,* 9 September 1966, p. 37.

Keim, Jean. *La Tour Eiffel.* Paris: Editions Tel, 1950.

Le Corbusier. *L'Art Décoratif d'Aujhourd'hui.* Paris: Les Editions G Cres et Cie., 1925.

Le Grain-Eiffel, René. Speech at centennial of first Eiffel viaducts. Château de Rochefort, Gannat, 16 August 1969.

_____. "Gustave Eiffel et son Oeuvre." Speech at opening of Lycée Technique Gustave Eiffel in Bordeaux, 26 November 1970.

Lindbergh, Charles A. *The Spirit of St. Louis.* New York: Charles Scribner's Sons, 1953.

Mandell, Richard D. *Paris 1900: the Great World's Fair.* Toronto: University of Toronto Press, 1967.

Maupassant, Guy de. *La Vie Errante.* Paris: Ernest Flammarion, Editeur, 1925.

McCullough, David. *The Great Bridge.* New York: Simon and Schuster, 1972.

McWhirter, Norris and Ross. *The Guiness Book of Records.* 12th U. S. ed., New York: Sterling Publishing Co., 1973.

Mock, Elizabeth B. *The Architecture of Bridges.* New York: The Museum of Modern Art, 1949.

Morlaine, Jacques. *La Tour Eiffel Inconnue.* Paris: Librairie Hachette, 1971.

Mumford, Lewis. *Sticks and Stones.* New York: W. W. Norton & Co., 1924.

_____. *The Brown Decades.* New York: Harcourt, Brace and Co., 1931.

"Now Man Conquers Mt. Eiffel." *Life*, 5 June 1964, pp. 108-10.

"L'Ouverture de L'Exposition." *Le Figaro*, 7 May 1889.

"Paris Recalls Building of 'Loathsome' Eiffel Tower." *Life*, 3 July 1950, pp. 2-4.

Peissi, P. *Eiffel*. Paris: Editions du Verger, 1946.

Picard, Alfred. *Exposition Universelle Internationale de 1889 à Paris. Rapport Général*. Paris: Imprimerie Nationale, 1891.

Poirier, René. *The Fifteen Wonders of the World*. New York: Random House, 1961.

Poncetton, François. *Eiffel, le Magicien du Fer*. Paris: Editions de la Tournelle, 1939.

Prévost, Jean. *Eiffel*. Les Editions Rieder, 1929.

Reports of the United States Commissioners to the Universal Exposition of 1889. Washington: Government Printing Office, 1890.

Rousselet, Louis. *L'Exposition Universelle de 1889*. Paris: Librairie Hachette et Cie., 1890.

Rudorff, Raymond. *Belle Epoque: Paris in the Nineties*. London: Hamish Hamilton, 1972.

Schneider, Pierre. "Paris: Timely Requiem for Les Halles." *The New York Times*, 25 May 1970, p. 42.

Shirer, William. *The Collapse of the Third Republic*. New York: Simon and Schuster, 1969.

Simon, Maron J. *The Panama Affair*. New York: Charles Scribner's Sons, 1971.

Skinner, Cornelia Otis. *Elegant Wits and Grand Horizontals*. Boston: Houghton Mifflin Co., 1962.

Sondern, Frederic, Jr. "Monsieur Eiffel and His Wonderful Tower." *The Reader's Digest*, June 1954, pp. 103-107.

Tuchman, Barbara W. *The Proud Tower*. New York: The Macmillan Co., 1966.

Vizetelly, Ernest Alfred. *Paris and Her People under the Third Republic*. London: Chatto & Windus, 1919.

Vogel, Robert M. "Elevator Systems of the Eiffel Tower 1889." *United States National Museum Bulletin*, no. 228, 1961.

Weil, B. *Panama*. Paris: Grasset, 1934.

White, Palmer. *Poiret*. London: Studio Vista, 1973.

Notes

ONE: A FAIR FOR FRANCE

[1] Terms of settlement. Cobban, pp. 10-11.
[2] "Divided us least." Shirer, p. 35
[3] As early as 1878. *L'Exposition de Paris 1889*.
[4] "The participant who can show . . ." Braibant, p. 18.
[5] Crystal Palace. Fitch, pp. 140-150.
[6] Six million visitors. This and other attendance figures for world's fairs are from Information Document 767 issued by the Bureau International des Expositions, Paris.
[7] "We will show our sons . . ." *L'Exposition de Paris 1889*, p. 11.
[8] Prospectus. *L'Exposition de Paris 1889*, p. 11.
[9] Proposals for tower. Eiffel, *La Tour Eiffel en 1900*, pp. 1-2.
[10] $1.6 million. Eiffel's estimate was 8 million francs. According to the Banque de France, the exchange rate at that time was 5.18 francs to the dollar; as a general rule I have rounded this to five in calculating dollar figures throughout the book.
[11] Eiffel's case against masonry. *La Tour Eiffel en 1900*, p. 3.
[12] Advantages of iron. Eiffel, *Les Grandes Constructions Métalliques*.

TWO: "USELESS AND MONSTROUS"

[1] Eiffel's contract. Picard, Vol. 2, p. 267.
[2] "To raise to the glory . . ." Braibant, p.223.
[3] Artists' protest. *Le Temps*, 14 February 1887.
[4] Léon Bloy. Keim, p. 7.
[5] Lockroy's reply. Picard, pp. 270-271.
[6] Hoover shocked English lady. Furnas and McCarthy, p. 33.
[7] Eiffel's reply. *Le Temps*, 14 February 1887.
[8] Sullivan concluded. Condit, *Skyscraper*, p. 44.

THREE: GLORIOUS TIMES FOR ENGINEERS

[1] Term Industrial Revolution. Hobsbawm, p. 28.
[2] "Glorious times." Hobsbawm, p. 168.
[3] "If we want any work done . . ." Furnas and McCarthy, p. 34.
[4] "The 19th century saw three great . . ." Fitch, pp. 140, 167.
[5] "The most profound . . ." Condit, *American Building*, p. 76.
[6] Jenny at Centrale. Condit, *Skyscraper*, p. 37.

7 Eiffel's ancestry, biography and early career. Eiffel, "Généologie de la Famille Eiffel; Biographie Industrielle et Scientifique," unpublished, completed in 1923.

8 "They're very amusing." Poncetton, p. 60.

Four: Master Builder in Iron

1 "What I need . . ." Poncetton, p. 100.

2 "The architecture of the future." Mumford, *Brown Decades*, p. 104.

3 Tay Bridge disaster. Poirier, pp. 228-229.

4 Eiffel's bridges and other projects. "Travaux de M. G. Eiffel et Principaux Ouvrages Exécutés par ses Etablissements de 1867 à 1890." Appendix to *La Tour Eiffel en 1900*, pp. 323-345.

5 "One of the victories . . ." Mumford, *Brown Decades*, p. 102.

6 Statue of Liberty. Description of building the statue in Handlin, pp. 28-48.

7 Great builders. Poirier, p. 247.

8 "He was pained . . ." Le Corbusier in preface to Cordat, *La Tour Eiffel*.

Five: The Tower Rises

1 All details in my narrative of the tower's construction are from Eiffel's definitive account, *La Tour de Trois Cents Mètres*.

2 "In almost every case . . ." Vogel, p. 2.

3 "It is curious and interesting . . ." Poncetton, p. 176.

4 Stop construction. Braibant, p. 83.

5 "The Tower is Sinking!" Poirier, p. 255.

6 "I was standing at a height . . ." Poirier, p. 252.

7 "Joined by belt of girders . . ." *La Tour de Trois Cents Mètres*, p. 108.

8 International Interoceanic Canal Study Conference. Bouvier, pp. 35-36.

9 Status of Eiffel's work on canal. Poncetton, p. 239.

10 "Judging by the interest . . ." Poncetton, p. 186.

Six: Technical Challenge

1 As in the preceding chapter, details of construction are from *La Tour de Trois Cents Mètres*.

2 A lucid explanation of the tower's elevators and the state of the art is given by Vogel, "Elevator Systems of the Eiffel Tower 1889."

3 Otis' telegram to Eiffel. Vogel, p. 28.

4 "Not only safe . . ." Vogel, p. 30.

Seven: *"Gloire à Monsieur Eiffel!"*

1 "Indian file, with M. Eiffel . . ." *L'Exposition de Paris 1889*, p. 58.

2 Eiffel's ideas on tower's scientific uses. *La Tour Eiffel en 1900*, pp. 17-19.

[3] "Was it simply the weather . . ." Braibant, p.76.
[4] "Fruit of intuition, of science . . ." Le Corbusier in preface to Cordat.
[5] Flag raising and Eiffel's speech. *La Tour de Trois Cents Mètres*, pp. 311-312.

EIGHT: FAIR STAR

[1] Opening of Exposition. *Le Figaro*, 7 May 1889.
[2] "Although this splendid result . . ." *Reports of the United States Commissioners to the Universal Exposition of 1889*, "Report of the Commissioner-General," pp. 9-10.
[3] *Song of the Century. L'Exposition de Paris 1889*, p. 82.
[4] Total admissions to tower. *La Tour Eiffel en 1900*, p. 34.
[5] Edison's note to Eiffel. Reproduced in facsimile in *La Tour de Trois Cents Mètres*.
[6] "Here we are all citizens . . ." *L'Exposition de Paris 1889*, p. 287.
[7] "Beginning in early morning . . ." Maupassant, *La Vie Errante*, p. 9.

NINE: WORLD ON DISPLAY

[1] The most comprehensive description of the fair is in *L'Exposition de Paris 1889*.
[2] "The resulting fortuitous assembly . . ." *Reports of the U. S. Commissioners*, "Report of the Engineer," p. 55.
[3] "In comparison   " "Report of the Engineer," p. 55.
[4] "One of the most striking facts . . ." *Reports of the U. S. Commissioners*, "General Review of the Sixth Group," p. 10.
[5] "The timbre of voice . . ." *L'Exposition de Paris 1889*, p. 309.
[6] "One of the most prodigious advances . . ." *L'Exposition de Paris 1889*, p. 310.
[7] "Buffalo Bill, who will be our guest . . ." *Le Figaro*, 16 April 1889.
[8] "Each nation, gradually losing . . ." *Reports of the U. S. Commissioners*, "General Review of the Sixth Group," p. 8.
[9] "I must demand supervision . . ." *Le Figaro*, 15 April 1889.
[10] "A painting . . ." Rudorff, p. 94.
[11] "Here has been shown the glorification . . ." *Reports of the U. S. Commissioners*, "Report of the Commissioner-General, p. 19.
[12] "This coincidence of the celebration . . ." "Report of the Commissioner-General, p. 20.
[13] "We have been only too inclined . . ." *Le Figaro*, 28 October 1889.
[14] "Everything connected with the Exposition . . ." *Reports of the U. S. Commissioners*, "Report of the Commissioner-General, p. 27.
[15] Quotations from the fan were taken directly from a photograph of it made available to the author by Henriette Venot.

TEN: BELLE EPOQUE OR FIN DE SIÈCLE?

[1] "A new idea in Europe." Quoted by Hobsbawm, p. 241.

[2] "I hope you may come to know . . ." White, p. 17.

[3] "I'd be very stupid . . ." Skinner, p. 9.

[4] "You arrived at your café . . ." Skinner, p. 94.

[5] "The harsh smell of gasoline . . ." Skinner, p. 7.

[6] "Where luxury is raised to a science." Quoted in Rudorff, p. 33.

[7] Number of brothels. Rudorff, p. 64

[8] "As an artist . . ." Quoted by Shirer, p. 107.

[9] "At one's feet . . ." Quoted by Shirer, p. 43.

[10] Bennett naked on Champs Elysées. Hawkins, p. 19.

[11] "The permanent glamour of France." Tuchman, p. 171.

[12] French birth rate. Vizetelly, p. 5.

ELEVEN: SCANDAL OF SCANDALS

[1] "A mechanism so simple . . ." Poncetton, p. 237.

[2] "The day will come . . ." Simon, p. 3.

[3] "This man who has lied . . ." Simon, p. 102.

[4] "There are two categories of Deputies . . ." Simon, p. 107.

[5] "The scandal of scandals . . ." Bouvier, p. 7.

[6] "You all know . . ." Simon, p. 126.

[7] Eiffel's statement to judge. Poncetton, p. 236.

[8] General Février's statement to Eiffel. Eiffel, "Biographie," pp. 38-40.

[9] "An American canal . . ." *Encyclopaedia Britannica*, Vol. 17, p. 172.

TWELVE: CAREER'S CREATIVE END

[1] Eiffel's early experiments are described in his *Travaux Scientifiques Exécutées à la Tour de Trois Cents Mètres.*

[2] "On rising by elevator . . ." *La Tour de Trois Cents Mètres*, p. 303.

[3] "During my engineering career . . ." Eiffel, "Biographie," Vol. 3, p. 1.

[4] Santos-Dumont's flight around tower. *La Tour Eiffel en 1900*, pp. 260-266.

[5] Early aviation experiments and wind tunnels. *The American Heritage History of Flight*, pp. 80-81.

[6] Bell's speech on presenting Langley Medal. "An Account of the Exercises," pp. 9-12.

[7] "Even in thick fog." Poncetton, p. 271.

[8] Eiffel's honorary decorations. Eiffel, "Biographie," Vol. 3, pp. 53-54.

[9] "Symbol of force . . . incomparable monument . . ." Eiffel, "Biographie," Vol. 1, pp. 44, 46.

[10] Description of Eiffel's town house and life there. Author's interview with René Le Grain-Eiffel.

11 $14 million by 1890. *La Tour de Trois Cents Mètres*, Appendix, p. 4.

12 Eiffel's study reconstructed at Salleboeuf. Author's visit there with Henriette Venot.

13 "I ought to be jealous of the tower . . ." René Le Grain-Eiffel.

14 "Eiffel's voice was soft . . ." Le Corbusier in preface to Cordat.

15 "The illustrious engineer . . ." *Discours Prononcés a l'Inauguration*, p. 34.

16 "From my father I inherited . . ." Author's interview with René Le Grain-Eiffel.

THIRTEEN: *LA GRANDE DAME*

1 "The Crusaders seeing Jerusalem's walls." Quoted by Collins and Lapierre, p. 236.

2 Sarniguet's race to top. Author's interview with Sarniguet.

3 Germans seized tower June 14, 1940. Information provided by Société Nouvelle d'Exploitation de la Tour Eiffel (SNTE).

4 Destruction of elevator systems. Information provided by SNTE.

5 Ingles' letter to Salles. Shown to author by Madame André Granet.

6 American soldiers on tower. Bryan, pp. 19 et seq.

7 Number of visitors to tower. SNTE documentation.

8 Tower admissions compared with other French monuments. Provided by French National Tourist Office.

9 Income figures for tower. SNTE documentation.

10 "Tower could have fallen into American hands . . ." *Le Figaro*, 28 February 2002.

11 Painting the tower. SNTE documentation.

12 Debate over tower's color. *Le Figaro*, 3 May 1968.

13 "Tower Razed?" "Tower in Good Health." *Le Monde*, 10-11 October 1972.

14 Renovation of tower, new lighting. SNTE documentation.

15 Citroën advertising on tower. Citroën public relations office.

16 Lindbergh sights tower. Lindbergh, p. 487.

17 20,000 flashing lights. SNTE documentation.

FOURTEEN: COMEDY AND TRAGEDY

1 Comte de Lambert's flight. *L'Illustration*, 23 October 1909.

2 Up tower on stilts. Braibant, p. 180.

3 Footrace. Braibant, also Cook, Don. "Landmark on the Seine." *Saturday Evening Post*, 11 August 1962, pp. 26-29.

4 Bicycle on stairs. Morlaine, p. 112.

5 Hugues Richard record. SNTE documentation.

6 Up on one leg. *Le Figaro*, 4 June 1959.

7 Collot crashes. Morlaine, p. 115.

[8] Moriarty fun. SNTE documentation.

[9] German student climbs. *Le Figaro*, 9 July 1954.

[10] Mountain climbers on 75th anniversary. Genêt in *The Yorker*, 16 May 1964; also *Life*, 5 June 1964.

[11] Hackett bungee jumps. SNTE documentation.

[12] Palmer drives, Petit walks. SNTE documentation.

[13] Ski slope. *L'Aurore*, 12 September 1969.

[14] First suicide. Braibant, p. 181.

[15] Teichelt's suicide. Morlaine, p. 107-110.

[16] Woman leaps from third platform. Braibant, p. 181.

[17] Incorrigible suicide. Morlaine, pp. 131-133.

[18] Change of mind. Morlaine, pp. 131-133.

[19] Woman lands on car. Morlaine, p. 129.

[20] "All three would be ugly . . ." *Le Figaro*, 14 October 1964.

[21] April Fool's jokes. Morlaine, p. 122.

[22] Fire on tower. *Le Figaro*, 4 January 1956.

[23] Smoke and flames at top. *The New York Times*, 23 July 2003.

[24] Prussian con man 1891. Braibant, p. 180.

[25] Lustig "sells" tower. Johnson and Miller book on the subject.

[26] NLF dynamite attempt. *Le Figaro*, 24 September 1958.

[27] SAO bomb plans. Braibant, p. 182.

[28] Muslim hijackers. *The Washington Post*, 27 December 1994.

[29] "Threat is real." *Le Figaro*, 21 October 2002.

[30] Belgian document shows Muslims target tower. *Le Figaro*, 19 September 2001.

[31] Bomb alert. *Le Monde*, 2 October 2001.

[32] 50th anniversary. Morlaine, p. 99.

[33] Automobile to 35 millionth visitor. *Le Figaro*, 1 July 1959.

[34] Letters to the tower. Shown to author by tower officials.

FIFTEEN: UNIVERSAL SYMBOL

[1] Antenna near Fargo. Information from station KTHI-TV.

[2] Baker's project for Wembley. Braibant, p. 167.

[3] Chicago tower project. *La Petite Architecture*, 1 November 1932.

[4] Miami tower project. SNTE.

[5] Importing Eiffel Tower to Myrtle Beach. *Atlanta Constitution*, 22 January 1974.

[6] Las Vegas Eiffel Tower copy. *The New York Times*, 12 September 1999.

[7] Watchmaker's model tower. *Le Figaro*, 21 September 1971.

[8] Howard Porter's model. Author's interview with Mr. Porter.

[9] Roger Blough's remarks; text on plaque. Public relations department, United States Steel.

[10] John Hancock Skystone. Public information department, John Hancock Mutual Life Insurance Company.

[11] "The surprising thing . . ." Barthes, p. 73.

[12] "Notre Dame represents the Faith . . ." *Le Figaro*, 30 December 1971.

[13] "A cage of bluebirds." Morlaine, p. 138.

[14] "Hello world . . ." Quoted by Braibant, p. 191.

[15] "I can hear the Eiffel Tower . . ." Quoted by Poirier, p. 238.

[16] Giraudoux on the tower. Quoted by Braibant, p. 189.

[17] "In 1911 Delaunay did . . ." Quoted by Morlaine, p. 137.

[18] "European civilization . . ." Speech to conference, "Les Valeurs Européennes," Strasbourg, July 1962.

[19] Roland Barthes on the tower. Barthes, pp. 27, 28, 33, 43, 60, 82.

[20] Maurice Besset on the tower. Besset, *Eiffel*.

[21] "The profound relationship . . ." Poncetton, p. 219.

[22] "The Eiffel Tower has entered . . ." Le Corbusier, *L'Art Décoratif d'Aujourd'hui.*

[23] "I bear witness to the tower . . ." Le Corbusier in preface to Cordat.

Index